SAINTS AND THEIR EMBLEMS IN ENGLISH CHURCHES

ST. LEGER AND ST. APOLLONIA
Painted screen-panels in Ashton Church, Devonshire

SAINTS AND THEIR EMBLEMS IN ENGLISH CHURCHES

BY

R. L. P. MILBURN

Fellow and Chaplain of Worcester College
Oxford

BASIL BLACKWELL

OXFORD

1961

First printed by the Oxford University Press, 1949
Revised Edition reprinted by Photolithography, 1957
Reprinted 1961

PRINTED IN GREAT BRITAIN FOR BASIL
BLACKWELL & MOTT LTD. BY THE COMPTON
PRINTING WORKS (LONDON) LTD. LONDON, N.I.
AND BOUND BY
THE KEMP HALL BINDERY, OXFORD

CONTENTS

FOREWORD

PERSONS who gaze about an ancient church will often notice, wrought in glass or stone or painted on screen panels, representations of saints—apostles, it may be, or bishops or virgin-martyrs—regularly distinguished, the one from the other, by a characteristic emblem. St. Peter has his keys, St. Laurence his gridiron, St. Blaise his fuller's comb, and so on, and these emblems serve clearly to identify the saint even when, as is often the case, the figure lacks inscription or title. The purpose of this handbook is to provide a list of such emblems as occur in English churches together with short biographies of the saints to whom the symbols belong. Other saints have been added who, whilst lacking a characteristic emblem, are sometimes portrayed in medieval churches or had churches anciently dedicated to them,[1] though it has not been thought necessary to mention a few names, such as Briavel or Egelwine, which, if not actually corrupt, belong to personages now entirely unknown. The saints commemorated in the Anglican calendars of 1662 and 1928 have been included also, while an Appendix treats of the angels, prophets, and sibyls who were sometimes closely associated with the saints in their task of declaring

---

[1] A few popes and bishops who appear only in a long series of ecclesiastics in the windows of such cathedrals as York and Wells have been allowed to pass unnoticed, and no account has been taken of the interesting figures to be found in the foreign glass, usually of Flemish or German origin, that was eagerly collected by nineteenth-century squires.

the manifold glory of God. On the other hand, most of the numerous but shadowy band of Celtic saints to whom churches are dedicated in Cornwall and other western counties have been omitted, not in any derogation of their merits, but for three reasons. They are more naturally linked with Wales or Ireland than with England, they pass unnoticed by the medieval artist,[1] and many of them are but local worthies, priests or missioners or anchorites, around whose unremembered lives has been woven a complex of fanciful detail that demands specialized study. In this matter, as on many other points of British hagiology, Miss Arnold Forster's *Studies in Church Dedications* (Skeffington, 1899) proves a valuable aid.

Most of the books which deal with the subject of saints and their emblems are based on F. C. Husenbeth's *Emblems of Saints*, the last edition of which was published in 1882 for the Norfolk and Norwich Archaeological Society and is now hard to come by. Husenbeth, however, included Continental as well as English examples; similarly, Maurice and Wilfred Drake in their sumptuously produced but not always accurate *Saints and their Emblems* (Werner Laurie, 1916) and even Francis Bond in his most useful *Dedications of English Churches* (Oxford University Press, 1914) give emblems not to be found in this country and therefore apt to confuse the amateur. The standard work of reference on the Lives of Saints, though it has little to offer on their emblems, is Alban Butler's collection, revised and augmented by H. Thurston and D. Attwater (Burns, Oates, and Washbourne, 1926–38). Those who wish to delve

[1] With one or two exceptions, such as St. Neot.

deeply into such matters may be drawn on to study the classic works of Émile Mâle, *L'Art religieux en France* (4th edition, Paris, 1940) and K. Künstle, *Ikonographie der christlichen Kunst* (Freiburg, 1926).

I have not attempted to disentangle variant traditions concerning a saint or to make nice distinctions between truth and falsehood, and the amount of space devoted to particular saints often corresponds rather with their medieval popularity than with their relative importance when judged by the sober standards of dispassionate historians.

R. L. P. M.

WORCESTER COTTAGE,
    OXFORD.

9 *February*, 1948

INTRODUCTION

THE common run of medieval people received their instruction in life and manners not from books but from pictures, and particularly from the pictures which met their eyes week by week and perhaps day by day in their parish churches. The arts of painting and statuary were seen in their full magnificence only in the great abbeys and cathedrals, yet few of even the humblest churches were so mean that they had not a few stained windows and carved figures to show. The craftsman might display his skill by illustrating the favourite stories from the New Testament as well as those Old Testament scenes—Noah and the Ark, Moses lifting up the serpent in the wilderness, Elijah in his fiery chariot, and the rest—which seemed to prefigure the events of the New Dispensation; but many churches were embellished principally with figures of saints, each standing alone, correctly habited in accordance with his calling as bishop or abbot or king or knight, and often holding some object which recalled a miraculous exploit or the manner of an heroic death. In time these emblems became so conventional that it was readily possible for the pious churchman, as he stood before a 'storied window', to identify the figures therein represented, even when no name or inscription was added, and thus to be reminded of the effective patronage of these saints and their power for weal or woe. For medieval art had a practical end rather than a concern with speculation and aesthetic theory. The saints were shown forth not as abstract figures, like Faith, Hope, and Charity, but rather as men and women who, revered and held in affection by their contemporaries, had now passed through death to a fuller life which enabled them to extend to their devotees in every age the favours with which God had allowed them to benefit mankind during their earthly lives. As active patrons and protectors they have their honoured place in the art of an age when beauty flowed naturally from devotion and all culture rejoiced in being the handmaid of religion.

'Saints': The Meaning of the Word

In his letters to the churches St. Paul sometimes adopts an expression from the Old Testament scriptures and greets the Christian converts as 'saints'[1] because they are members of the New Israel, the consecrated society established under the New Covenant. It was a matter of calling rather than of character, and St. Paul did not claim for his 'saints' at Ephesus or Rome or Corinth any pre-eminence in virtuous achievement, though it is assumed that Christian privileges imply an obligation to Christian conduct. The author of the Book of Revelation, however, writing at a time when the churches were encompassed with difficulties and persecution, paints a more vivid contrast between those who, yielding in time of trial, had fallen away to idolatry and the 'patience of the saints, they that keep the commandments of God and the faith of Jesus'.[2] The saints, as men deserving special honour, are linked with the apostles and prophets[3]

[1] Romans i. 7; 1 Corinthians i. 2; Ephesians i. 1.
[2] Revelation xiv. 12.   [3] Ibid. xviii. 20.

and bidden to join in exulting over the destruction of the corrupt pomp of 'Babylon'. They are, in fact, coming to be identified with the martyrs who, as an early letter from the church of Smyrna declares, are 'loved as the disciples and imitators of the Lord'.[1] Already, by A.D. 150 or thereabouts, the anniversaries of their martyrdom—the 'birthday' on which they were born into a higher life—were observed with diligent piety, and their bones, 'more valuable than jewels and more precious than gold',[2] were reverently bestowed in a tomb which often became a focus of devotion and the scene of miracles. Each church drew up its own list of martyrs, but some of them enjoyed more than a domestic reputation and soon found a place in the calendars even of remote cities. Thus St. Augustine, when preaching a sermon[3] about the Spanish deacon St. Vincent, was able to announce, with only a slight touch of exaggeration, that Vincent's heroic death was worthily commemorated in every church throughout the world. As time passed and the age of official persecutions came to an end, other virtues besides the heroic steadfastness of the martyrs gained recognition, and famous bishops or hermits were enrolled, along with the martyrs, in church calendars and honoured with the now formal title of 'saints'. The first of those who won their place in the list of 'men to be reverenced and imitated'[4] did so simply by reason of popular choice. Christians who had witnessed the noble death of a martyr or marvelled at the patient piety of some un-

---

[1] *Martyrdom of Polycarp*, xvii.
[2] Ibid., xviii.   [3] Number 276.
[4] Augustine, *Concerning True Religion*, 55.

usually devout monk proclaimed his worthiness to be commemorated for ever in the church which he had adorned, and, with the approval of the bishop, the cult of a new saint was thus adopted. But the growing tendency towards a centralization of ecclesiastical authority, together with a few examples of injudicious enthusiasm for somewhat unworthy pretenders to sanctity, caused canonization to become a papal prerogative. The matter is put concisely in a monition issued in 1479 by Laurence Booth, archbishop of York, forbidding the veneration of an image of King Henry VI: 'We must not call anyone a saint or accord him public veneration however excellent his life has been nor must we make any offerings to him openly and in public until this same person has received the approval of the Church and the Pope of Rome and has had his name inscribed in the list kept by the Pope.'[1] And so elaborate and expensive did the process of canonization become that Henry VI never received the honour to which popular fervour entitled him, since King Henry VII declined to pay the necessary fees.

Patron Saints

It may be convenient to set out some of the stages whereby the saints came to occupy so dominant a place in the unreflecting thought of the Christian worshipper as even to usurp divine prerogatives.

Emphasis on the majesty of God 'high and lifted up'[2] tends to remove Him from the easy grasp of the humble worshipper who then gladly avails himself

[1] This document is printed in W. H. Hutton's *The English Saints*, pp. 162-3. [2] Isaiah vi. 1.

of the intercession of 'friends at court'—the saints who, for all their mortal failings, have won a place around the heavenly throne. From time to time the voices of theologians were raised in protest at this lack of faith in God's benevolent providence. Thus, to take a fourth-century example, Hilary the Deacon, in his commentary on St. Paul's epistle to the Romans,[1] protests that 'people approach a king by means of officials and courtiers for the reason that a king is a human being and does not know to whom he ought to entrust political responsibility, but there is no need of an advocate in order to win the favour of God, from whom, after all, nothing is hid (for he knows the deserts of all men): what is required is a devout mind'. And, about the same time, a Spanish priest named Vigilantius incurred the savage hostility of St. Jerome for declaring that people should address their devotions to God rather than to the martyrs and 'pray for each other while they are alive'[2] instead of after death. Nevertheless, the view that came to prevail was an adaptation of earlier pagan ideas to a Christian form. The Greek poet, Hesiod, had described the men of the Golden Age as 'kindly, deliverers from harm, guardians of mortal men and givers of wealth',[3] and similarly beneficent powers were ascribed by popular enthusiasm to celebrated soldiers or statesmen who were hailed by one city or another as effective patrons. Thus, the townsmen of Amphipolis honoured the Spartan general Brasidas by carefully protecting his tomb and by paying him the compliment of sacrifices and annual games.[4] In much

---

[1] i. 22.   [2] Jerome, *Against Vigilantius*, 6.
[3] *Works and Days*, 122.   [4] Thucydides, *History*, v. 11.

the same way special reverence for martyrs was inculcated by the theory, no less than by the practice, of the early Christian church. Theodoret, a scholarly bishop of Cyrrhus, in Syria, quoted[1] Hesiod's lines about the men of the Golden Age and then added by way of commentary:

Now if the poet described those persons who lived really excellent lives as 'noble, averters of evil, guardians of mortal men', why does anyone condemn the practice of Christians? For we, in like fashion, acclaim as 'averters of evil and healers' those who were distinguished for devotion and met their death on that account. We do not call them 'divine'—may such mad folly ever be far from us!—but we speak of them as 'friends and servants of God' who use their free access to Him for the kindly purpose of securing for us the abundance of good things which they promise.

This power of the saints to intercede for those still upon earth is stressed by St. Ambrose, who exhorted his hearers to call upon the martyrs for aid:

They can ask pardon for our sins, since they washed away their own sins, if they had any, in their blood. They are God's martyrs, our advocates, the witnesses of our lives and deeds. We must not be ashamed to beg them to intercede for our weakness, since they knew the weakness of mortal flesh, though they overcame it.[2]

The medieval fathers used similar language. Thus St. Bonaventura, referring to the meritorious service of God upon earth which has won for the saints an exalted place in heaven, adds that they have obtained not merely blessing and glory for themselves but

[1] In his treatise, *A Cure for Pagan Ills* (viii. 915), written about A.D. 440.   [2] *On Widowhood*, ix. 55.

also the power to help others,[1] and St. Thomas Aquinas explains that

since prayer offered on behalf of others proceeds from charity, the more perfect the charity of the saints in heaven the more readily they pray for wayfarers who can receive benefit from their prayers, and the more closely they are united to God the more effective are their prayers; for the Divine Order is of such a kind that lower beings receive an overflow of the excellence of higher beings just as the air receives an overflow of the brightness of the sun.[2]

This belief that in the saints the worshipper possessed sympathizers, well acquainted with human frailty, but, because of their merits, powerful advocates with God, led on to the opinion that particular saints interceded most naturally and readily for those places and causes which had been dear to them during their lifetime. As early as A.D. 386 St. Gregory of Nyssa, a careful and somewhat academic theologian, could proclaim concerning a local martyr, St. Theodore, 'this, as we believe, is he who, throughout the past year, has calmed the raging of the barbarians and stayed the terrible onslaught of the fierce Scythians',[3] and he ended his panegyric with the appeal

Intercede for your country with our King and yours. For the country of a martyr is the place where he suffered, and his fellow-citizens and kinsfolk are those who have cherished him and guard his remains and honour him. We fear tribulations, we await dangers, the loathsome Scythians are near at hand and plotting war against us. Fight for us as our champion; since you are a martyr, plead freely with God on behalf of your fellow-servants.

[1] *Sentences*, iv. 45. 3. ii.
[2] *Summa Theologica*, II. ii. 83. 11.
[3] *Sermon on St. Theodore the Martyr*, iii. 737.

Paulinus of Nola, a fifth-century bishop and poet, related that the emperor Constantine, when founding his new capital city, formed the 'inspired plan' of importing the remains of St. Andrew from Greece and St. Timothy from Asia Minor,

> That so he might protect his city walls
> With apostolic bodies, and be safe;[1]

and such beliefs had become so firmly grounded before long as to cause the Romans to leave part of their city wall unfortified, even when the Gothic army was threatening an onslaught, because they were confident that the Apostle Peter would continue to protect the place which he held in especial affection.[2] The choice by cities of a particular saint as patron was often emphasized by a change of name which might serve to bind the place ever more closely to its protector. Thus the small French town of Briovère commemorated its saintly bishop Lo, whose relics it jealously guarded, by abandoning the old title and adopting the name St-Lo, and, in England, names such as St. Albans and St. Ives likewise testify to a proud regard for a local hero.

But sometimes the interest of the saint was assumed to be vocational rather than local, in that he became patron not of a place but of a guild. Members of the guild were commonly those following the trade which the saint had pursued during his lifetime, as when shoemakers put themselves under the protection of SS. Crispin and Crispinian and domestic servants looked to St. Sitha for help and mediation. Or

[1] *Poems*, xix. 335.
[2] So, at least, the historian Procopius says (*On the Gothic War*, i. 23).

again, the saint might be chosen for a rather incongruous association of the manner of his death with the implements used in a particular calling. Thus St. Blaise, whose flesh had been torn by an iron comb, became patron of the wool-carders and, in more questionable taste, St. Bartholomew, who had met his death by flaying, was selected to be patron of the tanners. Individuals also hastened to seek the peculiar protection of a saint who would represent them in the heavenly places. Bishop Dionysius of Alexandria bears witness to the fact that, as early as A.D. 260, sons of Christian parents were often called 'Paul' or 'Peter', and he maintained that 'there have been many persons bearing the same name as John the Apostle, who, because of their love and admiration and respect for him and because they desired to be loved by the Lord, as he was, were glad to be named after him'.[1] And the custom of bestowing upon children the names of saints pre-eminent for virtues and thus enjoying high favour with God became more and more popular as the principle gained acceptance that men 'thereby secure for their children a firm refuge and protection'.[2] Within a century of his execution St. Laurence is found performing such kindly offices as answering the prayer of a certain Satyrus, who whilst on a visit to Sicily was struck down by illness, that he might return alive to his home at Milan,[3] or granting to a Florentine woman named Juliana the gift of a son. He showed himself, in fact, to be the sort of advocate whom the Spanish hymn-writer

[1] Eusebius, *Ecclesiastical History*, vii. 24. 14.
[2] Theodoret, *A Cure for Pagan Ills*, viii. 923.
[3] Ambrose, *On the Death of Satyrus*, i. 17.

Prudentius might reasonably and hopefully implore to 'hear a rustic poet when he confesses the sins of his heart and acknowledges his misdeeds'. 'Well do I know', Prudentius continues 'that I am not worthy to be heard by Christ himself, yet, with the martyrs as my patrons, I can obtain healing.'[1] Especially would the need of such powerful intercessors be felt at the 'great and terrible Day' of Judgement at the end of the world when ordinary mortals, vividly conscious of their failings, would tremble before the majesty of Christ. 'Make the martyrs', urged Pope Gregory the Great, 'your patrons when you stand your trial before the stern Judge; summon these to defend you in that dread day. . . . The holy martyrs are at hand to protect us; they like to be entreated and, if I may put it so, they seek to be sought after';[2] or, to turn to Prudentius once more and hear his prayer to St. Vincent, 'Be present now and hearken to the voice of our supplication, thou who canst stand before the Father's throne and plead with success on behalf of guilty mortals.'[3] And sometimes, in medieval pictures of the Last Judgement, the Virgin Mary is shown standing beside the scales in which a human soul is being weighed against its misdeeds and putting out her finger to incline the balance, as it trembles, towards salvation.

The theologians draw a careful distinction between the honour that is paid to the saints and the adoring worship which is properly offered to God alone, but popular devotion, in language and in sentiment, frequently outran the sober definitions of scholars and

[1] Prudentius, *Peristephanon*, ii. 574.
[2] *Homilies on the Gospels*, ii. 33. 8.   [3] *Peristephanon*, v. 545.

approximated closely to a polytheism which from time to time aroused the mockery of the heathen and the protests of the faithful. The saints, in fact, ministered to the same kind of religious need as the pagan genii of mountains, valleys, and forests had done, and eager pilgrimages were made to their tombs. It had been the opinion of Plato that souls bound down by sensuality were unable to break away from their earthly chains and 'wandered about the monuments and tombs',[1] and this association of the departed spirit with the place where its body lay was extended in a later age to all souls and, in particular, to the noblest of all—the heroes of paganism or the Christian saints. The Roman poet Tibullus, when rejected by his mistress, vows that he will hasten to the tomb of her dead sister: 'I look on her as divine: to her tomb will I bring gifts and garlands wet with my tears; to her grave will I fly and, seated as a suppliant before it, I will bewail my fate to her silent dust.'[2] Tibullus' lament, though its tone is artificial and less than half-serious, bears witness to the current belief that prayer at the tombs of the departed was of singular efficacy. The Christian worshipper, therefore, would hasten in his distresses to a shrine which enclosed 'inestimable treasure', as the people of Antioch described the bones of St. Ignatius, on the principle that 'God, ever glorifying his own even after their death, works strange wonders at their tombs and resting places'.[3]

One reason for the popularity of visits to the tombs

---

[1] Plato, *Phaedo*, 81c.   [2] II. vi. 31.
[3] Bishop Asterius of Amasea, *In Praise of the Holy Martyrs*, 325.

of the martyrs was that sudden and inexplicable healings did, as a matter of fact, quite often take place there. When every allowance has been made for exaggeration and credulity, the abundant records of miraculous cures, effected before witnesses, cannot be dismissed as imaginary. Whether the recipients of these benefits were correct in assigning their new-found happiness to the intercession of the saints is a matter, perhaps, for argument and speculation, but most medieval people, while not without a streak of curiosity and even scepticism in their character, readily accepted miracles as part of the established order of things and rejoiced, with St. Chrysostom, that 'not the bodies only but the very tombs of the saints are full of spiritual grace'.[1] Hence the interest taken in shrines and relics. St. Augustine staidly maintained that

one must not spurn or neglect the bodies of the dead and particularly the bodies of those just and faithful persons whom the Spirit used as instruments and vessels for all good and holy purposes. A garment or a ring or anything of this kind which belonged to a father is valued by his children in proportion to the love they had for him. So the bodies themselves are on no account to be disregarded since they are obviously far more a part of a man's real self than any garments could be.[2]

Thomas Aquinas deduced from this passage the proposition that the bodies and even the small personal possessions of the saints should be highly respected, on the ground that bodies which have been united with God in good works and martyrdom are holy

[1] *Sermon on St. Ignatius the Martyr*, 5.
[2] *City of God*, I. xiii.

and endowed with a sanctifying influence whilst the objects, insignificant in themselves, which have been dear to the saints should be dear also to the faithful followers of the saints. Of course, scandals and abuses sometimes occurred, as when the unscrupulous partisans of one monastery shamelessly stole relics belonging to another. For instance, St. Withburga was buried in her nunnery at East Dereham, but the fate of her body after death ill matched the placid piety of her life, since the monks of Ely were so racked by envy that they prevailed upon King Edgar to allow them to claim Withburga's corpse and then, fearing that the precious relic would not lightly be given up, had resort to violence and subterfuge. The abbot of Ely arranged to hold court at East Dereham and arrived there attended by a considerable retinue. A night of feasting was brought to a close by the announcement that the monks must retire to church for their devotions, but, in fact, they busied themselves less with their prayers than in abstracting Withburga's coffin. The loss was soon discovered by the townsfolk of Dereham who went in pursuit but, failing to catch up with the monks before they reached the fenland swamps, they had the mortification of seeing the successful thieves heading for Ely in the only boats which were available. And critical minds, long before the days of Erasmus and Calvin, could point to certain ridiculous features in the cult of relics, as when two monasteries, stirred perhaps rather by avarice than by piety, claimed possession of the same relic and exhibited it to the faithful as genuine. Thus the scholarly Guibert of Nogent, offended by the assertion that the head of John the

Baptist was preserved both at Angers and at Constantinople, was moved to exclaim: 'Now what more absurd story could be told about that heroic man than that these two lots of people should make him out to be a double-headed monster?'[1] But the ordinary churchman did not pause to reason the matter out in terms of sophisticated attack or defence. For him the churches erected over the tombs of the martyrs—St. Peter or St. Agnes at Rome, St. Edmund or St. Thomas in England—derived interest and sanctity from the presence within them of such hallowed remains, so that a keen sense of devotion coupled with a lively hope of benefits both temporal and eternal drove him to 'goon on pilgrimages'.[2]

And when people returned from journeying to distant shrines

> The holy blisful martir for to seke
> That hem hath holpen, whan that they were seke,[3]

as well as when they had to content themselves with offering their prayers at home, they never tired of seeing, in the windows of their church, representations of the saints whom they regarded as their protectors, together with the pictures or symbols that recalled the victories which these patrons had won over the Devil.

Church Dedications: the Choice of Saints

Moreover, the churches themselves were usually dedicated to a saint or saints. On this subject there is little to add to the observations of Richard Hooker

[1] *On Relics of the Saints*, I. iii. 2. Cf. *Gesta*, I. v.
[2] Chaucer, *Canterbury Tales*, prologue, 12.
[3] Ibid.

who, in his *Laws of Ecclesiastical Polity*,[1] defends this
practice against his Puritan opponents. 'Touching
the name of Angels and Saints whereby the most of
our churches are called; as the custom of so naming
them is very ancient, so neither was the cause thereof
at the first, nor is the use and continuance with us at
this present, hurtful.' After emphasizing that 'churches
were consecrated unto none but the Lord only',
Hooker continues 'and because the multitude as of
persons so of things particular causeth variety of
proper names to be devised for distinction sake,
founders of churches did herein that which best liked
their own conceit at the present time; yet each in-
tending that as oft as those buildings came to be
mentioned, the name should put men in mind of
some memorable thing[2] or person'. He quotes St.
Augustine:[3] 'The nations to their gods erected
temples, we not temples unto our Martyrs as unto
gods, but memorials as unto dead men whose spirits
with God are still living.' Hooker is aware that
not everyone has observed Augustine's delicately
balanced distinctions, and that superstition and error
have from time to time corrupted the reverence due
to the martyrs, but he concludes:

Divers considerations there are, for which Christian
churches might first take their names of Saints: as either
because by the ministry of Saints it pleased God there to
show some rare effect of His power; or else in regard of
death which those saints having suffered for the testimony

[1] v. 13; published in 1597.
[2] By 'thing' Hooker means dedication to Wisdom or Peace,
such as was made at Constantinople and elsewhere in the East
by some of the emperors.   [3] *City of God*, viii. 10.

of Jesus Christ did thereby make the places where they died venerable; or thirdly, for that it liked good and virtuous men to give such occasion of mentioning them often, to the end that the naming of their persons might cause inquiry to be made, and meditation to be had of their virtues.

Since it was by their works that the saints commended themselves, surprising comparisons occur in their popularity as patrons. Many heroic martyrs, devout scholars, and prudent administrators of the early Church—Ignatius, Polycarp, Clement of Alexandria, Cyprian, Athanasius, Basil, John Chrysostom—are very seldom depicted by English artists of the Middle Ages or honoured by church dedications, whilst such others as Christopher, George, or Margaret of Antioch, whose very existence is not wholly free from doubt, became the objects of keen interest and reverence, thus influencing both literature and art. For repute as helpers was required rather than importance in secular or, indeed, in ecclesiastical history, and the healing of a demoniac or the stilling of a tempest outweighed any successes that lacked the divine hallmark of miracle. But a variety of reasons led to the selection of a particular wonder-worker. The choice of the Twelve Apostles, the 'pillars' on which the Church was founded, is natural enough, and they were often shown holding scrolls inscribed with a sentence from the Apostles' Creed, which they were thought to have composed while assembled in solemn conclave shortly before they separated for their world-wide mission. Again, the patron saint of a church was often represented in its windows or on its screen, while in the side-chapels, where trade guilds met for their services, the patron saint of the guild usually appeared. Moreover, local patriotism ensured that in each diocese those saints were honoured with warm affection who had, in their day, trodden the field paths and village streets known to their medieval venerators. It is, therefore, on the rood-screens of Norfolk that King Edmund and St. Walstan and St. William of Norwich are to be seen, whereas Devonshire favours St. Sidwell and Yorkshire St. William of York or John of Bridlington, and a series of windows in the church of St. Neot, Cornwall, illustrates the life of the somewhat obscure saint who gave his name to the place. The influence of the Roman see is shown by the appearance in English churches and English calendars of not only such notable martyrs as Laurence and Sebastian but also a number of lesser figures—St. Faith and St. Prisca, for example—whose cult was popular at Rome. Lastly, the donors who paid for the windows often had reasons of their own for choosing out one saint rather than another for illustration. The saints whom they regarded as their own personal protectors had an obvious claim, and St. James might be selected, or St. Martin, in gratitude for a successful pilgrimage to Compostella or Tours. Occasionally a donor seems to have taken a sophisticated pleasure in presenting an academic collection of recondite saints, as when Isabel of Ingoldisthorpe embellished the north aisle of the church at Wiggenhall St. Mary Magdalene, Norfolk, with a window that exhibits such little-known personages as Felicianus, Januarius, Prosdocimus of Padua, and Romanus of Rouen.

The Sources and Character of Traditions concerning the Saints

The traditions concerning the Christian saints were drawn from a variety of sources. Sometimes, as with John the Baptist or Stephen, the books of the New Testament provided sufficient material, while the Apocryphal Gospels, though they failed to secure for themselves a place in the canon of sacred Scripture, supplied the details about such saints as Joachim and Anne. Other life stories were derived from the straightforward chronicles of contemporary historians of whom perhaps the most notable representatives are Eusebius of Caesarea in the fourth century and the Venerable Bede in the eighth. Again, many of the accounts were drawn from the so-called 'Acts (*Acta*) of the Martyrs', documents which claimed to be straightforward records of the questioning and condemnation of those who declined to yield either to the threats or to the blandishments of Roman governors and join in the ceremonies of pagan worship. The genuine examples of official reports, to which nothing has been added beyond the necessary minimum of explanatory comment, are distinguished by the concise and objective tone that is proper to a legal précis,[1] but they are greatly outnumbered by those Acts of the Martyrs which are to be classed rather as eyewitness descriptions. Records of this class, such as the *Martyrdom of Polycarp*, offer much contemporary information of high value, but their usefulness varies in accordance with the reliability of the narrator—and anyone who has ever

[1] As, for instance, the 'Acts' of St. Cyprian.

attended a court of law will realize the differences between man and man in the faculty of accurate observation. Another group of 'martyr-acts' consists of official records or eyewitness accounts which have been subjected to free editing in an effort to improve the story or point a moral. This embellishment of a bare account may be studied best in the case of certain 'Acts' which exist in a number of different versions, each one embroidered and developed in accordance with the varying exuberance of the storyteller's enthusiasm.[1] Lastly, there are 'Acts' which, though retaining an appearance of formal accuracy, are, in fact, the product of the historical imagination playing upon a few sketchy details or which are simply fictions designed to edify the faithful or, on occasion, to enhance the reputation of an unknown saint and thus glorify the monastery which guarded his relics. Moreover, such 'uncertain stories', as Cranmer called them in his Preface to the 1549 Prayer Book, served not only to instruct but also to amuse. They were the novels of the Middle Ages, and the fable, for instance, of St. Julian Hospitaller is the counterpart of *Tess* or *Barchester Towers* rather than the unvarnished chronicle of a particular life. And, just as the patterns of fiction are reproduced again and again with but slight variations, so a single legend may attach itself to many names. St. Marina is said to have been a pious woman who was clothed by

---

[1] The story of the pious St. Procopius, which is simple and straightforward enough as it is concisely told by Eusebius in his *Martyrs of Palestine* i, suffers such varied exaggeration in later legendaries as to be almost completely transformed into several diverse accounts.

her father in the habit of a monk and accompanied him when he retired to a monastery. She there sustained with great patience the malicious accusation that she was the father of a bastard child, and suffered expulsion from the monastery. After long years of enforced penitence she was allowed to return, but died shortly afterwards. Then, as she was being laid out for burial, it was discovered that she was, in fact, a woman and therefore incapable of the sin that had been alleged against her, 'whereat all were astonished and feared, and knowledged that they had trespassed greatly in the servant of God'.[1] Thus runs Marina's story, but it is told also, with a few differences in detail, about Eugenia, Euphrosyne, Pelagia, and Theodora.

'So long as history was regarded as an art, the sanctions of truth and accuracy could not be severe', observed Professor J. B. Bury in an address given at Cambridge in 1903, and those who wrote up the lives of the saints as an 'eternal possession'[2] of the faithful did not always feel bound to a strict observance of the distinction between fact and fantasy. Not, indeed, that the men of the Middle Ages were indifferent to exact knowledge and detailed history, though the events which appealed to the savant and his readers as important were far from being such as would normally attract a modern journalist. The thirteenth century, at any rate, was an age in which studious churchmen rejoiced to bring their new-found learning 'in subjection to Christ' and elaborated vast encyclopaedias to declare the variety and interest of

[1] *Golden Legend*, translated by Caxton, iii. 228.
[2] Thucydides, i. 22.

the world that God had made. Perhaps the most monumental of such works of detailed and all-embracing scholarship is the *Mirror* of Vincent of Beauvais. This 'glutton for books', as he was nick-named by his contemporaries, arranged his rich store of material in four parts, which he called the Mirror of Nature, the Mirror of Instruction, the Mirror of Morals, and the Mirror of History. In the Mirror of Nature the varied members of Creation are reviewed —the elements, vegetable and animal life and, in particular, Man, to whom dominion over nature has been entrusted. The Mirror of Instruction recounts the story of the Fall and declares man's need of a Redeemer. But it explains also that through work and knowledge man may prepare himself for salvation, and the manifold branches of knowledge and crafts-manship are discussed. The Mirror of Morals points to virtuous action as the objective alike of life and of learning, and supplies a detailed classification of virtues and vices. Finally the Mirror of History traces the course of events from the lifetime of Abel to the year 1253. Though he offers little exegetical comment, Vincent of Beauvais makes it clear from his arrangement of facts that the expectation of the Old Testament heroes as well as all the splendour of pagan culture finds fulfilment only in the Christian dispensation and that it is the triumphs of Christian character rather than the rise and fall of empires which possess abiding significance. Therefore, in his great conspectus of history, the events which Vincent describes at length are not military or political but religious. The collapse of dynasties and the warfare of nations are dismissed in a few lines, but the courage of the saints, the austere discipline of monks, the renunciations of hermits, and the miracles which a detachment from earthly things enabled such persons to perform are told with a fullness of detail which bespeaks devoted enthusiasm.

It was stories of this kind which delighted the ear and satisfied the mind of people high and low, simple or cultured, in the Middle Ages, and details of the life and achievements of each saint came to be collected from various sources and written up in the 'lectionaries',[1] from which appropriate extracts were read in church on the feast-day of a martyr. In these legends history tends to repeat itself with a certain monotony. For when, as often happened, merely the name of a particular saint and the fact of his martyrdom were known, the pious curiosity of the faithful was satisfied from a common tradition in which, as in Victorian melodrama, black is black and white is white and both heroes and villains, deprived of individuality, display the typical characteristics of prodigious virtue or prodigious vice. Sometimes the theme varied, and the faults of the saints were magnified in order that the wonders of the divine, reforming grace might be made manifest, but, as a rule, the martyrs are notable for resolute faith, calm courage, and unyielding chastity while the Roman emperors and provincial governors emulate Nero in senseless savagery. It is here not a case of the falsification of narrative but rather the filling in of inevitable gaps with conventional portraiture. The author of the prologue to the *Martyrdom of St. Fortunata* struck a

---

[1] Later incorporated in the breviaries, or books used in the recitation of the canonical hours of prayer.

somewhat sophisticated note of critical detachment when he observed, 'The Martyr-acts of the saints enjoy comparatively little authority for the reason that in them falsehoods are found mixed up with the truth': most of his contemporaries were happy enough to accept the fanciful embroidery along with the bare facts and follow St. Bernard's belief that 'our weakness is aided by the intercession of the saints, our heedlessness is shaken when we consider their blessedness and our ignorance is instructed by the patterns which they provide'.[1]

The Golden Legend

The fullest and best collection of the much-loved stories concerning the saints was made about A.D. 1270 by Jacobus de Voragine, a Dominican friar who became archbishop of Genoa. His *Legends of the Saints* soon gained the title of the *Golden Legend* on the ground that 'in like wise as gold is most noble above all other metals, in like wise is this Legend holden most noble above all other works'[2] and came to enjoy high repute throughout western Europe. Before 1340 it had been translated from Latin into French by Jean de Vigny and on this French version Caxton's English edition of 1483 was based, with, however, the addition of a few Biblical stories and the lives of some national saints, such as Cuthbert, Alban, Alphege, Dunstan, and Swithun who had passed unnoticed in the original *Golden Legend*.

[1] The second *Sermon on All Saints' Day* (Migne edition, *P.L.* clxxxiii. 463).

[2] Caxton's Introduction, following the French of Jean de Vigny.

There was no startling originality in de Voragine's work. What he did was to draw from the lectionaries, add a number of legends from the verbose encyclopaedias of such men as Vincent of Beauvais, and write up the whole in a compact and vigorous manner, thus popularizing stories which had hitherto been, for the most part, easily accessible in the liturgical books alone.

The great majority of scenes from the life of a revered patron-saint that were shown forth in the windows of a medieval church could be explained by reference to de Voragine's authoritative collection, which, though rich in edification and steeped in homely piety, provided also excitement and bizarre adventure. The characters of the stories contained in the *Golden Legend* are drawn from every walk of life and display their saintly heroisms in a colourful variety of dramatic situations. Men of every calling could set before themselves examples of sanctity displayed by earlier courtiers, physicians, cobblers, beggars, and the rest, who thus revealed the possibilities of any human life, whether spent in exalted or in circumscribed conditions. On the other hand, the *Golden Legend* had tales to tell of remote lands and unknown peoples, thus transporting the stay-at-home citizen of London or York to India with St. Thomas or, in the company of St. Antony, to the burning sands of the Egyptian desert. But more highly appreciated than the scraps of history and geography were the miracles. Tastes change from age to age and whereas, in our day and generation, we value, both for interest and for truth, stories which wear a sober, everyday aspect, to the medieval reader such narratives appeared feeble and monotonous when placed by the side of tales which were embellished with savage dragons, fantastic tortures, and evil magicians. Not, indeed, that the whole *Golden Legend* wears an air of Arabian Nights fantasy. The lives of some of the Western saints—in particular such bishops as St. Lambert—are related with a staid conciseness typical of the sober chronicles from which the accounts were drawn. But Jacobus de Voragine, and other collectors of legends, felt an excited interest also in those heroes of the Eastern Church whose biographies had been written up, in the full exuberance of Oriental imagination, on the principle that a man is proved holy in accordance with the extent of the supernatural powers which God bestows upon him or manifests on his behalf. And even the saints of England or France or Italy wrestled with 'principalities and powers', winning their victories, by the help of angels, over malevolent demons. Earth and Heaven meet, but the transitory things of earth are far less important than the substantial realities of Heaven and Hell.

The Origin of Emblems of the Saints

The medieval Christian, then, liked to read about the exploits of his patrons and to see them depicted in his churches, most of which contained a representation of St. Christopher bearing the Holy Child on his shoulder, St. Martin dividing his cloak with the beggar, or, it might be, St. Nicholas raising to life the three children whom the innkeeper had slain and cast into a pickling-tub. Often, however, the artist was commissioned to paint or carve the figure only, and had neither space nor opportunity to illustrate an accompanying scene, and, in that case, one bishop was indistinguishable from another and it was impossible to decide whether a virgin martyr was St. Agatha or St. Agnes or St. Barbara or St. Dorothy. The custom, therefore, arose of placing under the saint's feet or, more commonly, of putting into his hands a distinguishing emblem—the axe or spear with which he met his death or else some object which recalled his most famous miracle. By the end of the fourteenth century these emblems had, with the help of the *Golden Legend*, been largely standardized in western Europe, and in this way a ready means of identification was provided with the natural result that each saint became connected in popular belief with the incident, whether martyrdom or miracle, thus concisely symbolized. Sometimes the conventional emblems were misunderstood and themselves gave rise to legend. When saints such as Denis, Osyth, and Sidwell were shown holding their heads in their hands, this crude but vigorous representation was at first intended to do no more than remind the worshipper that these martyrs were decapitated. Proudly and serenely they enter the gates of Heaven bearing their mutilated heads rather than the sword which was the instrument of their death. But fertile imaginations were allowed to play upon these pictures, and the story grew up that St. Denis had carried his head in his hands from Montmartre to his place of burial and that St. Osyth calmly walked, after her execution, to the spot which she had selected for her grave. Another example of mistaken interpretation is supplied by the snake or dragon which regularly symbolized pagan idolatry. The emperor Constantine caused a painting to be made of himself piercing this dragon with a lance, and some of the saints were similarly depicted to show that they had been energetic missioners in heathen lands. But, as the story of St. George shows, this allegorical dragon easily becomes a sinister creature of flesh and blood demanding its toll of human sacrifice from the city which it holds in thrall and being overcome only when supernatural powers are bestowed on some saintly deliverer. But the medieval faculty for weaving stories out of symbols is shown at its most exuberant in the case of St. Erasmus (Elmo). He was a favourite patron with sailors and his image adorned the prow of many ships that crossed the Mediterranean, with the result that he was sometimes depicted carrying a windlass with a rope coiled round it. He appears thus in the stonework which decorates King Henry VII's chapel in Westminster Abbey, but, by the time that statue was carved, the windlass bore a macabre significance. For it had come to be regarded as the means whereby Erasmus met his death, and the story gained wide acceptance that the saint had suffered, at the hands of his persecutors, the torment of having his stomach slit open and his entrails wound out by means of a windlass. Some emblems might thus be misconstrued and other emblems are no more than puns, as when Pope Cornelius bears a horn (*cornu*) or King Olaf (Holofius) carries a 'whole-loaf' of bread. A few symbols, again, are generic rather than particular, so that a book may be held not only by the four Evangelists but by anyone with pretensions to learning or with a notable devotion to Church services, a palm indicates victorious martyrdom,[1] and a sword witnesses to judicial execution. But the unity of aspiration and culture which characterized Western Christendom in the Middle Ages brought it about that, in many lands, the figures of the best-loved saints could be identified, even by the unlettered and the stranger, through the use of a common set of emblems which ensured that affectionate and unforgetful honour was paid to the 'friends of Christ, the children and heirs of God'.[2]

[1] Revelation vii. 9.
[2] John of Damascus, *On the True Faith* (Migne edition, *P.G.* xciv. 1164).

ACCA

Acca was a Northumbrian who sympathized with St. Wilfrid to the extent of sharing his exile and missionary journeys in Sussex and in Frisia. When Wilfrid was able to return to his diocese, Acca received the reward of his faithfulness by being appointed abbot of Hexham and, on Wilfrid's death in 709, Acca succeeded as bishop. He followed Wilfrid's example by enforcing Roman as opposed to Celtic usages throughout his diocese, and by his energy in building and adorning churches. He was also an enthusiastic patron of music and scholarship, establishing a library that was much appreciated by Bede. Acca was, for unknown reasons, deprived of his see in 732 and spent some years in Galloway, but he returned to Hexham before his death. He was buried there and revered by the monks as a saint, and is depicted on a screen-panel at Hexham in the vestments of a bishop but without any characteristic emblem.

ADELINE

Adeline won fame chiefly from her connexion with her pious and energetic brother, St. Vitalis, founder of the Cistercian Abbey of Savigny. Vitalis established a convent of 'White Ladies', with his sister as abbess, also in the forest of Savigny, but later caused it to be transferred to Mortain, in Normandy (about A.D. 1120). Neither brother nor sister attracted much attention in England, but the church of Little Sodbury, Gloucestershire, is dedicated to St. Adeline.

ADRIAN

According to his story in the *Golden Legend*, he was a young knight of Nicomedia who was converted by witnessing the steadfast confidence of Christians under torture during an outbreak of persecution about A.D. 304. On his refusal to perform pagan sacrifices he was imprisoned, whereat his wife Natalia, who had secretly embraced Christianity, 'ran to the prison and kissed the chains that her husband was bound with', encouraging him to remain firm in the faith. He endured savage tortures which culminated in his limbs being crushed on an anvil and then hacked off. St. Adrian was a popular saint in Europe and gained repute as a protector against plague, but is very rarely depicted in England. On the screen at Wolborough, Devon, he is shown with what appears to be his anvil.

AFRA

Afra suffered martyrdom at Augsburg, during the persecution of Diocletian, about A.D. 304. Her *Acts*, a late and unreliable composition, give a colourful story which makes her a courtesan who gave refuge to a Spanish bishop named Narcissus and his deacon. Under their influence she and the members of her household were converted to Christianity, whereat she refused to participate in pagan sacrifices and was burnt to death on an island in the river Lech. St. Afra, a patron of penitents, enjoyed great popularity in Germany during the Middle Ages, and is often portrayed on the Continent at the stake or with flames playing about her feet, but it is very doubtful whether the English figures that are described as 'St. Afra' have been correctly interpreted.

AGATHA

According to the story contained in the *Golden Legend* and based on her very dubious *Acts*, she was a wealthy virgin of Catania, in Sicily. She died in A.D. 251 as the result of imprisonment and torture inflicted upon her by the Governor Quintianus, when she refused his amatory advances and ridiculed his gods. Her breasts were cut off but miraculously restored, and she may, therefore, be represented holding a breast in a pair of pincers, or with a sword driven through her breasts. St. Agatha is venerated at Catania as the protectress of that city against the fires of Mount Etna.

AGATHO

Agatho, a Sicilian by birth, was pope of Rome A.D. 678–81 and gained high repute for his friendliness and serenity. Two events of historical importance occurred during his pontificate: he was instrumental in securing the condemnation, at a council held at Constantinople in 680, of the heresy which denied that Christ had a human will, and he supported St. Wilfrid's claim to be restored to the see of York from which he had been debarred by St. Theodore's reforming zeal. Agatho, who was celebrated at Palermo and at Rome as a worker of miracles, attracted little attention in England; but he is portrayed in a window of the choir at York Minster.

AGNES

Her legend, as related in several versions by St. Ambrose and others, makes her a girl who was put to death at Rome about A.D. 305, in the thirteenth year of her age. She declined to marry the son of the prefect of Rome and, when her clothes were stripped off, her hair miraculously grew long to provide a covering. She survived an attempt to burn her alive and was subsequently stabbed.

St. Agnes sometimes holds a sword, or stands with a sword driven into her neck, but her characteristic emblem is the lamb (*agna*) in her hand or lying at her feet, in punning allusion to her name. Her cult at Rome, where she was popularly regarded as a protectress of the city, is very ancient, and the present noble church of St. Agnes was constructed around her tomb, probably by the emperor Constantine, in the fourth century A.D.

AIDAN

A monk of Iona, he undertook the arduous task of evangelizing Northumbria and received the devoted help of Kings Oswald and Oswin. He was consecrated bishop in 635 and established his see at Lindisfarne (Holy Island), whence he made frequent journeys in order to preach the Faith far and wide and to found churches and schools. His prayers availed even to change the direction of the wind and thus to divert the fire which the heathen Penda of Mercia had kindled against the royal city of Bamburgh, while his acts of charity and humanity, such as the gift of his valuable horse to a needy beggar, won him unstinted praise from his contemporaries and from Bede, but failed to catch the imagination of the medieval artist. Aidan died in 651, 'leaving to his clergy', as Bede remarked, 'a most salutary example of abstinence' and 'having signally commended his doctrine by regulating his life in accordance with its precepts'.[1]

[1] *Ecclesiastical History*, iii. 5.

ALBAN

Reputed the earliest martyr of Britain. An influential and attractive knight, he was converted to Christianity by a Welshman named Amphibalus and, refusing to obey the command of the Caesar Maximian[1] (about A.D. 300) that he should sacrifice to Jupiter and Apollo, was beheaded at the city which now bears his name. Remarkable portents occurred at the time of his death, and the executioner's eyes dropped out. St. Alban's emblems are various, often a tall cross or a sword.

[1] So runs the *Golden Legend*; but it is not likely that Maximian intervened in British affairs, and Constantius Chlorus, who was then administering Britain and Gaul, appears to have been favourably disposed towards the Christians. This would not, however, necessarily prevent harsh action by local governors.

ALBINUS

Albinus (Aubyn) became abbot of the monastery of Tincillac, between Angers and Poitiers. In 530 he was appointed to the see of Angers and, during his twenty years as a bishop, gained great repute for his miracles of healing. One day, as Albinus was passing the prison at Angers, the prisoners appealed to him for help, 'wherefore he went to his church and soon after, his prayer made to God, kneeling before the high altar, a great part of the prison wall fell down and so escaped every prisoner there'.[1] St. Albinus, a popular patron in France and Germany, was little known in England, but is very occasionally depicted as a bishop, with no distinctive emblem.

[1] *Golden Legend.*

ALDATE

Aldate is perhaps the same person as Eldad, a Welsh-man who became bishop of Gloucester in the fifth century and, after showing great vigour in promoting resistance to the Saxon armies under Hengist, was slain in battle by the heathen invaders. Be that as it may, there are ancient church-dedications to St. Aldate at Gloucester and at Oxford, and his feast-day, 4th February, is regularly noted in the medieval service-books of western England. The calendars of such books entitle him 'bishop and confessor'.

Note: The suggestion that St. Aldate never existed and that his name is merely a corruption of 'Old Gate' ignores the fact that he had his dedications both at Gloucester and at Oxford by A.D. 1100 and possibly much earlier. Moreover, neither church was so close to the medieval gates as naturally to take its name from them, while the nearest gates were called not Old Gate but Northgate (Gloucester) and Southgate (Oxford). In general, where a church is distinguished, from others that are dedicated to the same saint, by some such explanatory addition as Colegate or Castlegate, it is the addition rather than the patron saint that tends to be dropped in the course of time. And at Oxford it was another church now demolished—St. Michael Southgate—which took its distinctive name from the only city-gate anywhere near St. Aldate's.

It would seem that Aldate is a real person, even though his identity with Eldad cannot be proved.

ALDHELM

After prolonged studies at Malmesbury and Canterbury he became abbot of Malmesbury about A.D. 675. He not only enriched his own abbey with new buildings but also established monasteries and monastic schools at Frome and Bradford-on-Avon. His classical learning was notable: he produced a work 'De laudibus virginitatis' as well as an elaborate treatise on Latin verse. Aldhelm became bishop of Sherborne in 705 and died in 709. Few representations of him remain and he has no symbol to distinguish him from other bishops. Three ancient parish churches are dedicated to him, as well as the chapel on the Dorset headland which bears his name.

ALEXIS

According to his legend, which first appears in the ninth century, Alexis was a Roman of noble birth who lived during the reign of the emperor Honorius (A.D. 395–423). He abandoned his wife, with her consent, on his wedding-day, and travelled in the East as a poor pilgrim for seventeen years. Becoming annoyed at the attention which his repute for holiness attracted, he set sail for Sicily, but the ship was blown out of its course and arrived at Rome. As a beggar, and unrecognized, he approached his father, who had pity on him and ordered that he should receive board and lodging with the servants of his household. The servants treated him badly 'and oft-times threw on him the washing of dishes and other filth' besides forcing him to make his bed under the staircase. But Alexis endured everything patiently and gave himself up to prayer and fasting for another seventeen years. When he realized that the end of his earthly life was drawing near, he arranged proofs of his identity and, after his death, his sanctity was proclaimed by a voice from Heaven. Though he enjoyed considerable popularity on the Continent as a patron, St. Alexis is seldom met with in England. He is shown on the rood-screen at Torbryan, Devon, holding a ladder, to commemorate his sojourn under the staircase.

ALFRED

The son of Ethelwulf, king of the West Saxons, he succeeded his brother Ethelred on the throne in 871. His reign was vexed by intermittent warfare with the Danes. In 878, after Alfred's victory at Ethandun, Guthrum, king of the Danes, consented to retire to the eastern half of England and to receive baptism, but the treaty was broken in 884 and, during the campaigns which followed, Alfred came to be accepted as the champion of England and of Christianity, and thus prepared the way for the union of all England under one sovereign. Alfred's biographer, Asser, ascribes to him an almost superhuman perfection. He is said to have devoted himself with unwearied zeal to the welfare of his people as legislator and as champion of the poor against oppression. By establishing a community of women at Shaftesbury and another of men at Athelney he strove to rekindle enthusiasm for the monastic life, and by encouraging scholars and founding schools he promoted sound education. In his desire to instruct his people, he took the trouble to translate, with copious explanatory notes, Boethius' *Consolation of Philosophy*, Bede's *Church History*, and other works. Alfred's life of manifold activity was dogged by ill health, and he died at the age of fifty-two in A.D. 901. He is shown as a king, with no distinctive emblem, in fifteenth-century glass formerly in the library but now in the ante-chapel of All Souls College, Oxford, while, in the statuary on the west front of the cathedrals at Exeter and Lichfield,[1] he bears a harp.

[1] The statue here is a modern imitation.

ALKELDA

Two Yorkshire dedications honour St. Alkelda, but the facts of her life are unknown and her existence has been doubted. She may have been put to death by Danish invaders, and stained glass formerly existing at Middleham, the supposed scene of her martyrdom, showed her being strangled.

ALKMUND

Five English churches are dedicated to St. Alkmund and his shrine at Derby gained high repute, but he is a shadowy figure. He is said to have been the son of Aelred, king of Northumbria, and to have been murdered by supporters of Eardulf, a claimant to the throne, in A.D. 800. Curiously enough Eardulf (or Hardulph) is honoured with a church dedication at Breedon-on-the-Hill, Leicestershire. He gained an undeserved reputation for sanctity because of a tradition that, when he had been executed by order of King Ethelred and his body had been laid out for burial near the Minster at Ripon, he suddenly revived and appeared within the Minster safe and sound.

Another Alkmund is portrayed on a screen-panel at Hexham. He succeeded St. Fridbert as bishop of Hexham (A.D. 767–80) but, though he was famed for sanctity of life, no detailed traditions about him have been preserved.

ALPHEGE

Whilst abbot of Bath he was appointed bishop of Winchester through the influence of St. Dunstan, who was eager to advance the interests of the Benedictine monks. In 1006 he was promoted to the archbishopric of Canterbury, but the times were troublous and, five years later, the Danes, led by Thurkill and Erdrith, took advantage of the enfeebled state of England under Ethelred the Unready to raid and plunder. Alphege, who had previously played an active part in persuading Olaf Tryggvesson, king of Norway, to abandon his alliance with the Danes and pursue a policy of neutrality, was taken captive to Greenwich where, since he refused to allow the Church to pay his ransom, he was stoned and then beheaded. His emblems, therefore, are stones or a battle-axe.

AMBROSE

One of the Four Doctors of the Western Church (the others being Jerome, Augustine, and Gregory), who not uncommonly appear on medieval screens and pulpits or, in stone, as pinnacles at the top of East Anglian church-towers. Ambrose, who showed great promise as a lawyer, became a magistrate at Milan, and when, in A.D. 374, the election of a new bishop was to take place, presented himself at the church in order to check any disturbance that might be caused through the rivalry of Catholics and Arians. But the cry was raised, 'Let Ambrose be bishop', and he was chosen by popular acclamation to occupy the see even though he was not yet baptized and was most reluctant to abandon his secular career. This seemingly capricious election was amply justified since Ambrose excelled as scholar, administrator, and hymn-writer, and was instrumental in securing the conversion of many inquirers, including St. Augustine, to the Christian faith. He is usually represented in episcopal vestments and without the beehive or the scourge which are his characteristic emblems on the Continent. The beehive commemorates the visit paid to him, as he lay in his cradle, by a swarm of bees which settled on his face and mouth and then flew away heavenward, while the scourge recalls the penance enforced by Ambrose upon the emperor Theodosius I after the massacre of seven thousand contumacious inhabitants of Thessalonica.

ANASTASIA

Several martyrs of this name are recorded, but traditions about them are confused and unreliable. The most famous Anastasia is said to have been imprisoned by her husband at Rome as a punishment for her zeal in visiting and encouraging Christian prisoners during times of persecution at the end of the third century. On his death she regained her liberty but was arrested shortly afterwards and banished to the island of Palmaria where she was burnt or, according to another version of the story, buried alive. Her name appears in the canon of the Roman Mass and she is reverenced by the Greek Church as 'Pharmacolytria'—the guardian-saint who renders poison ineffective, but very few representations of her remain in England. In glass dating from about 1440 at All Souls College, Oxford, she is shown wearing a blue tunic and a yellow and white cloak, but without any characteristic emblem.

ANDREW

After St. Peter, the most popular of the Apostles in medieval times, to judge from the number of churches (about 637) anciently dedicated to him in England. He does not play a very conspicuous part in the Gospel story, and his fame rested on his legendary *Acts* which told of missionary labours, signalized by miraculous healings, in Scythia and Greece, and of his crucifixion at Patrae, near the entrance to the gulf of Corinth, by order of a zealous Roman governor named Aegeas. Although there is nothing in his story to show that his cross was of other than the normal shape, his regular symbol is the cross saltire, perhaps to distinguish him from Christ and from St. Peter. The special connexion of St. Andrew with Scotland began in the eighth century when, according to tradition, some of his bones were secretly transferred from Greece to St. Andrews.

ANNE

According to a tradition first found in the apocryphal Gospel of St. James (about A.D. 160), the mother of the Virgin Mary was named Anne. She and her husband Joachim suffered great distress of mind because of their childlessness, but their prayers and lamentations were heard and an angel announced to Anne that she should bring forth a child who was to become famous throughout the world. Anne then vowed that the child should be devoted to the Lord and, when Mary reached the age of three, her parents pre-sented her with much ceremony in the Temple. In the later Middle Ages miraculous stories gathered round the name of St. Anne, but they came too late to have any effect on English church art and she is usually depicted teaching the Virgin to read.

ANSELM

A native of Aosta, he met with much harshness from his father and migrated to the monastery of Bec, in Normandy, where his sympathetic nature and refined scholarship soon led to his appointment as prior and, later, as abbot. In 1092 he went to England in order to assist in drawing up constitutions for the monks of St. Werburgh at Chester and was forced, much against his will, to accept the archbishopric of Canterbury. He defended the privileges of the Church against the demands of King William II with such tenacity that exile became inevitable and in 1097 he went, by way of Rome, to settle at the monastery of Telese, in southern Italy, where he was able to complete his treatise on the Incarnation. When William II died, in 1100, Anselm was invited to return to England and was received with the greatest enthusiasm, but within a short while he became involved in the quarrel between Henry I and Pope Paschal II on the subject of 'lay investiture'. Finally, in 1107, a settlement was effected, largely through Anselm's mediation, whereby Henry renounced the right for himself or any other layman to invest either bishop or abbot with staff and ring, while the Pope gave permission for prelates to do homage to the King as temporal ruler. Thereafter Anselm, in spite of ill health, devoted himself to his pastoral duties, to his vast correspondence with those from all parts of Christendom who sought his advice, and to the production of a treatise on Freewill and Predestination. He also vigorously defended the rights of the see of Canterbury to primacy in England against the pretensions of the archbishop of York. He died, worn out by his labours, in 1109 and speedily became a revered figure whose life was surrounded by an aura of legend. But St. Anselm was not formally canonized until 1494, and is very seldom depicted by medieval artists.

ANSKAR

A Benedictine monk of New Corvey, in Westphalia, he was selected to continue the missionary work in Denmark which had been started by Ebbo, archbishop of Rheims (A.D. 826). Harald, king of Denmark, had just received baptism at Mainz, and Anskar accompanied him on his return to Denmark, but Harald's tenure of the throne was contested and, after doing little more than establish a school where boys could be trained for ordination, Anskar crossed to Sweden, where he was allowed by King Björn to preach and teach freely. His success led, in 831, to his appointment as the first archbishop of Hamburg and as papal legate throughout Scandinavia. He sent Gauzbert to continue the evangelization of Sweden, whilst he himself toiled vigorously, though with scanty resources, in Denmark and Schleswig-Holstein. But the confusion which followed the death of the emperor Louis the Pious and culminated in the sack of Hamburg by piratical Danes in 845 brought this work to ruin. Anskar retired to Bremen whence, with courage and persistence, he strove once more to direct missionary expeditions to Sweden and Denmark, but, on his death in 865, little of permanence had been achieved there. St. Anskar remained practically unnoticed in England until the inclusion of his name in the calendar of the 1928 Prayer Book.

ANTONY

Antony (about A.D. 251–356) was celebrated for his long life of austere self-discipline in the Egyptian deserts and as one of the founders of Eastern monasticism. At the age of about twenty he was orphaned and, in literal obedience to the Gospel precept[1] 'If thou wouldest be perfect, go, sell that thou hast . . . and come, follow me', gave up his property to the poor and became a hermit, dwelling at first near the scattered cells of other anchorites but finally retreating farther from the haunts of man to a ruined castle near the Nile. Here he practised for twenty years a solitary routine of severe asceticism, varied only by the preaching of simple, practical sermons to the crowds who were attracted by his reputation for holiness. Antony emerged from his retirement to comfort the Christians of Alexandria during the persecution set on foot by the emperor Maximin in A.D. 311, and then, as the danger abated, withdrew to a still more secluded abode near the Red Sea where, however, he allowed himself the recreation of cultivating a vegetable garden. From time to time he paid visits to former disciples, but declined all invitations to preside over a monastery. St. Antony usually appears as a venerable, bearded figure,[2]

[1] St. Matthew xix. 21.

[2] The illustration is taken from a picture of St. Antony in fifteenth-century glass (partly restored) at Langport, Somerset, where he is, exceptionally, shown as quite a young man.

sometimes holding a **T**-shaped staff or bell and attended by a pig. The story grew up that the pig was his sole companion in the wilderness, but the real reason for Antony's emblems seems to be that he was patron of an order of Hospitallers founded in the south of France in A.D. 1095. These Antonines devoted their lives to the care of the infirm—hence the crutch—and enjoyed the privilege of being exempt from a police order which forbade men to allow their pigs to forage in the gutter—hence the pig.

APOLLONIA

Apollonia is described, in a quotation taken by the historian Eusebius[1] from a letter of Bishop Dionysius of Alexandria, as an 'aged virgin' who, in the persecution of the emperor Decius (A.D. 250), had her teeth broken with blows on the jaws and was afterwards burnt to death. Medieval representations, however, make her a maiden, by no means aged, holding pincers and a tooth, as though her teeth had been forcibly drawn out.[2] No church is dedicated to her in England, but she was popularly invoked to ward off toothache.

[1] *Ecclesiastical History*, vi. 41.
[2] See Frontispiece.

ARILDA

Her relics were treasured at Gloucester Abbey. She is said to have been beheaded by a tyrant named 'Muncius', but her history and date are quite uncertain. The church at Oldbury-on-Severn is dedicated to her.

ARMEL

Armel (Armagilus) migrated, with several companions, from south Wales to Brittany about A.D. 520. His attempt to establish a religious community was disturbed by the hostility of the usurper Conmor, but he enjoyed the protection of King Childebert and, after the death of Conmor, was able to found monasteries at Rennes and Ploermel. The most famous of his miracles was his victory over a dragon which was laying waste the country-side around Rennes. He bound the beast with his stole, led it to the top of a hill now called Mont-St-Armel, and commanded it to plunge into the river below. He is therefore depicted wearing a chasuble over armour and leading a dragon by a stole tied round its neck. King Henry VII, when in peril of shipwreck off the coast of Brittany, called upon St. Armel and was delivered from his danger, and a statue of the saint may be seen in Henry VII's chapel at Westminster Abbey.

ASAPH

A monk of St. Kentigern's great monastery on the banks of the River Elwy, he became noted for piety, learning, and miracles, and was appointed by Kentigern to succeed him as abbot, about A.D. 573. He was also consecrated bishop of the surrounding district which he cared for with such diligence that the name of the diocese was subsequently changed from Llanelwy to St. Asaph. He is occasionally portrayed in English churches, as in a fifteenth-century window at Torbryan, Devon, or on the brass of John Blodwell at Balsham, Cambridgeshire, where he appears as a bishop without distinctive emblem.

ATHANASIUS

Athanasius became secretary to Alexander, bishop of Alexandria, and accompanied him to the great Council of Nicaea in 325. The condemnation of the Arian heretics which took place there was entirely in accord with the ideas of Athanasius, who had already begun his series of treatises defending the Divinity of Christ. In 328 Athanasius was elected to the see of Alexandria, but he was involved in frequent controversy and his forty-five years as bishop were chequered by five periods of exile, during which he stayed at Trèves, at Rome, or with the monks of the Egyptian desert. Athanasius stands out as the foremost champion of Nicene orthodoxy against Arianism, whilst his philosophic insight and lucidity of expression have earned for him the title 'Father of Scientific Theology'. Moreover, his firmness, tempered with geniality, made him an ideal bishop in turbulent times, and he enjoyed widespread respect and affection in his diocese. Yet, in spite of his importance in the history of the Church, St. Athanasius was generally disregarded in the popular devotion of the Middle Ages. No ancient church is dedicated to him in England, and he is very seldom depicted; in the ante-chapel of New College, Oxford, he is shown as a bishop without distinctive emblem.

AUBERT. See HONORIUS

AUGUSTINE
OF CANTERBURY

Sent by Pope Gregory I at the head of a band of forty monks to effect the conversion of England, he was well received on his arrival in Kent by King Ethelbert, whose early acceptance of Christianity was of decisive importance towards influencing the attitude of the Kentish people towards the Roman missionaries (A.D. 597). Augustine took up residence at Canterbury whence he travelled far and wide proclaiming the Gospel message and, in defiance of the British bishops of the western Midlands, linking the Church of England with Rome rather than with such Celtic centres as Iona, from which the early missions to Northumbria had been sent out. St. Augustine is represented as a bishop, without any distinctive emblem.

AUGUSTINE OF HIPPO

(A.D. 354–430.) Classed with Ambrose, Jerome, and Gregory as one of the four Doctors of the Western Church he yet, in the words of the *Golden Legend*, 'surmounted all the other doctors of the church . . . , flourishing without comparison as well by example of virtues as by abundance of doctrine'. His *Confessions* have earned for him the affection, his *City of God* the respect, of successive generations. After a tempestuous youth, Augustine was converted to Christianity through the influence of his devoted mother, St. Monnica, and the reasoned arguments of St. Ambrose. When he returned to Africa, in A.D. 388, he went to live with some of his friends in a religious community at Tagaste, but his intellectual brilliance and pastoral enthusiasm caused his appointment as coadjutor-bishop to Valerius of Hippo and then his election to the see of Hippo when Valerius died in A.D. 396. Augustine soon came to be acknowledged as the pillar of orthodox Christianity, and the authoritative advice of his letters was accepted far and wide. His life was vexed by the theological controversies which caused him to produce his classic treatises on Grace and Predestination and by the decay of the Roman empire which exposed Africa to the dangers of civil war and the invasion of the Vandals, but, throughout these trials, Augustine preserved the confident steadfastness of one to whom the disasters of the present age serve mainly to emphasize the joys awaiting those who attain to the City of God set 'eternal in the heavens'. He is the reputed founder of the monastic order of Augustinian Canons.

Medieval artists often depict him wearing doctor's robes, but he may appear as a mitred bishop with no distinctive symbol. On the Continent he sometimes holds a burning heart in his hand, but this symbol of his fiery zeal is rarely met with in England.

BARBARA

According to the *Golden Legend*, she was a Syrian whose beauty was such that her father enclosed her in a tower to protect her from the attentions of importunate suitors. Barbara, however, exasperated her father by refusing the hand even of eminent princes and by ordering the workmen to insert three windows, symbolizing the Holy Trinity, in a cistern which her father had designed to have two windows only. She was brought before the judge and, refusing to sacrifice to idols, endured severe tortures, after which she was put to death by her father, who was thereupon struck by lightning. She is revered as patron against lightning, fire, and thunderstorms, and protects from sudden death. Her regular emblem is her tower.

BARNABAS

Barnabas is first mentioned in the Acts of the Apostles as a Cypriote who, having sold a field, 'brought the money and laid it at the apostles' feet'.[1] He was influential enough to be able to commend St. Paul to the Church at Jerusalem and, after working as a 'prophet and teacher'[2] at Antioch, was solemnly chosen, along with Paul, to undertake 'the first missionary journey'. When Lystra was reached, his dignity and stature so impressed the inhabitants that he was acclaimed as Jupiter.[3] After their return to Antioch, Paul and Barnabas became involved in the troubles concerning the circumcision of Gentile converts and went up to the council of Jerusalem, where their evidence helped to settle the matter. Shortly afterwards another missionary tour was planned, but when Paul opposed Barnabas, who wished again to take his cousin John Mark with them, a 'sharp contention'[4] arose and Barnabas, abandoning Paul, sailed away with Mark to Cyprus. There, according to a later tradition, he was stoned or burnt to death by the Jews. St. Barnabas is not often represented in medieval paintings, and has no characteristic symbol.

[1] iv. 36.   [2] xiii. 1.   [3] xiv. 2.   [4] xv. 39.

BARTHOLOMEW

In the Gospel story he is a name and no more unless he be identified with Nathanael, 'an Israelite indeed, in whom is no guile'.[1] But he enjoyed great popularity in the Middle Ages and some 165 churches are dedicated to him. His *Acts* recount missionary labours and the miraculous overthrowing of idols in India. 'Then all the bishops of the idols assembled them together and went to Astrages the king, and complained of the loss of their gods and of the destruction of their temples. And Astrages was wroth and sent a thousand men armed to take the Apostle.' The manner of his death is variously described, but the tradition prevailed that he was flayed alive and he is regularly depicted holding a flaying-knife. Some of the dedications to St. Bartholomew in Northumberland may be intended to honour not the Apostle but a twelfth-century Bartholomew who lived for forty-two years as a hermit on the island of Farne.

[1] St. John i. 45-51.

BASIL

Basil (A.D. 329–79) belonged to a family remarkable alike for culture and for piety. Two of his brothers, Gregory of Nyssa and Peter of Sebaste, as well as his sister Macrina, are canonized saints. After prolonged studies at Caesarea, Constantinople, and Athens, Basil became a professor of rhetoric at Caesarea in Cappadocia but, largely owing to the influence of Macrina, he decided to abandon a promising secular career and devote himself to studious asceticism. For two years he travelled far and wide in order to converse with hermits and learn their mode of life, and then chose a beautiful site on his estate at Annesi, in Pontus (Asia Minor), for the establishment of his monastery. Hitherto monks had lived alone or in groups that lacked any organization, but Basil drew up detailed rules for the men who were drawn by his charm and reputation to join him in a common life of work and prayer. His constitution is the norm of Eastern monasticism at the present day, and, since it was extensively drawn on by St. Benedict, has been influential in the West also. Basil was not allowed to pass all his days in peaceful contemplation, for he was persuaded from time to time to emerge as a champion of orthodoxy against the onslaught of the Arian heretics, while his practical charity was displayed when he sold all his possessions in order to provide relief during a famine. In 370 Basil was appointed archbishop of Caesarea and for nine stormy years he continued to labour, in the fields of administration and scholarship, to preserve and propagate the Faith. Like St. Athanasius and other great Fathers of the

Church, St. Basil gained no popularity as a patron-saint during the Middle Ages. He was neglected by English artists, and Toller Fratrum, Dorset, is his only church dedication.

BEDE

(A.D. 673–735.) From the age of eight until he died, Bede knew no other home than Jarrow Monastery, and his life was passed in an uninterrupted round of devotion and scholarship. His commentaries on Scripture and his scientific treatises show an unusual breadth of learning and sympathy, but far more valuable to-day is his *Church History* which offers detailed information about the spread of Christianity in England up to Bede's own day. His remains were stolen from Jarrow and carried off to Durham, where they were at first placed in St. Cuthbert's coffin and later enclosed in a splendid shrine in the Galilee porch. On the stand supporting the shrine was an inscription in monkish verse describing Bede as 'venerable',[1] and this probably helped to fix as his peculiar epithet a title which was applied with conventional politeness to many priests in Anglo-Saxon times. Bede is usually shown holding a book, but has no more distinctive emblem.

[1] Haec sunt in fossa
Bedae venerabilis ossa.

BEGA

Bega, the patron-saint of St. Bees, in Cumberland, has been identified with a nun named Begu who, according to Bede's *History*,[1] received a prophetic vision of the death of St. Hilda. More probably she was of Irish parentage: a late legend recounts that, in order to avoid a distasteful marriage, she fled across the sea and settled in a hermitage, passing her days in prayer and works of charity. When her solitude had been disturbed by pirates, she was appointed by St. Aidan to direct a small community of nuns established on the island of Cumbrae, in the Firth of Forth.

[1] iv. 23.

BENEDICT

(A.D. 480–543.) A member of a noble Umbrian family, he shrank from the demoralization of his times and retired as a hermit to Subiaco. His reputation for sanctity soon resulted in an invitation to preside over a neighbouring monastery but, being unable to inculcate godliness or discipline there, he returned to his cave and gradually established twelve small communities made up from the devout disciples who sought his counsel. About A.D. 530 he transferred to Monte Cassino and for the monks who followed him there he drew up a detailed rule of life. This Benedictine Rule became the norm of Western monasticism, and the establishment of later orders of monks usually denotes an attempt to observe it with greater zeal and precision. Benedict became renowned for his insight into the hearts of men and for a forcefulness of character which allowed him boldly to rebuke Totila, the victorious king of the Ostrogoths, as well as to repel satanic powers which, according to report, rose up against him in material form. He is depicted by medieval artists as an abbot, holding a crozier with which he sometimes repels devils howling at his feet.

The church known as St. Benedict's, at Glastonbury, was originally dedicated to St. Benignus, the companion of St. Patrick. The tradition ran that Patrick set out from Ireland to visit Glastonbury, whereat Benignus followed in search of his master and took it as a sign that his quest was about to be successful when the staff which he was holding suddenly burst into leaf.

BENEDICT BISCOP

(A.D. 628–90.) An Anglo-Saxon of noble birth, he held an honourable post at the court of King Oswy of Northumbria, but decided to abandon his secular career and set out on a pilgrimage to Rome. He met St. Wilfrid on the way: they journeyed together and both became enthusiastic supporters of Roman as opposed to Celtic Christianity. Benedict returned to Northumbria and then, after another visit to Rome, became a monk on the island of Lérins, off the south coast of France. In 668 Pope Vitalian appointed him to accompany Theodore, the newly elected archbishop of Canterbury, to England. Benedict was detained at Canterbury, where he became abbot of St. Peter's, and then went to Rome once more to buy books. Returning to Northumbria he enjoyed the enthusiastic patronage of King Egfrid and, with his assistance, established a monastery on the Roman model at Bishopwearmouth. Benedict took great pains to secure skilled masons and glaziers for the work as well as in providing an expert teacher of plain-chant and a notable collection of books and vestments for the benefit of the monks; and he was scarcely less diligent in his arrangements for the foundation of a second monastery at Jarrow. He died after a long illness which he faced with exemplary cheerfulness and patience. St. Benedict Biscop was seldom portrayed by medieval artists: when he appears, as at Wintringham, Yorkshire, he has no emblem except an abbot's crozier.

BERNARD

(A.D. 1091–1153.) At the age of twenty-two he abandoned the career which his rank as a Burgundian noble laid open to him and eagerly embraced the life of a Cistercian monk, surpassing all others in the intensity of his devotion and the strictness of his asceticism. In 1115 he was chosen to be abbot of the new foundation at Clairvaux, and the charm of his eloquence drew great numbers of men to enter the monasteries of his Order. From his many theological treatises, which display mystical insight as well as controversial ability, St. Bernard gained the title of 'the mellifluous doctor', but nowadays he is better remembered as the author of such hymns as *Jesu dulcis memoria*. He was active both in promoting the authority of Pope Innocent II and in preaching the Second Crusade, while exceptional powers of counsel and healing were attributed to him. Some of St. Bernard's miracles, such as the occasion when he cursed and thus slew a swarm of flies which was infesting a newly built church, are illustrated in medieval German glass now at St. Mary's, Shrewsbury. Elsewhere he is not commonly depicted. When he appears, it is as an abbot, sometimes accompanied by a dog. The occurrence of the dog is due to the story that, a little while before Bernard's birth, his mother dreamed that she was holding in her arms a white dog with a black back, these colours being prophetic of the habit later adopted by members of the Cistercian Order.

BERTOLINE

Bertoline (Bertram) was an anchorite who established himself in the eighth century at Irlam, Staffordshire, where his shrine may be seen to this day. According to a late and unreliable tradition, Bertoline was a Mercian prince who crossed over to Ireland in his desire to escape the temptations which surrounded him at his father's court. He ran away with an Irish princess but, when she and her child were devoured by wolves, he was filled with sorrow and penitence, and gave himself up to a life of the strictest asceticism. After a sojourn at Stafford, where he was received unsympathetically by the king, and was miraculously preserved from harm in a contest with the king's champion, he moved on to a more secluded hermitage at Irlam. The church at Barthomley is dedicated to him, and formerly he had a church at Stafford also.

BIRINUS

Birinus was sent by Pope Honorius in 634 to evangelize those districts of central England that had not yet been visited by any other missionaries; but, when he discovered that the inhabitants of Wessex, where he landed, were still pagan, he remained there instead of pressing on farther. Receiving help and encouragement from King Cynegils of Wessex, who was one of his first converts, he established an episcopal see at Dorchester (Oxon.) and gained renown for his zeal both as pastor and as builder of churches. Some medallions of thirteenth-century stained glass at Dorchester show St. Birinus in the vestments of a bishop, with pastoral staff and mitre, but he lacks any distinctive emblem.

BLAISE

Bishop of Sebaste, in Asia Minor, he met his death during the persecutions started by the emperor Diocletian (about A.D. 300). His legend relates that he was beheaded after he had been torn with iron combs. Blaise therefore appears, in medieval representations, as a bishop holding a large comb, and he became patron saint of wool-combers. His festival was celebrated with considerable splendour at Bradford even as recently as 1825, and in the course of the pageantry he was eulogized in verses beginning

> Hail to the day whose kind, auspicious rays
> Deigned first to smile on famous Bishop Blaise.

St. Blaise was also invoked to ward off diseases of the throat, because of the story that his prayers saved a boy, who had a fishbone stuck in his throat, from choking to death.

BLIDA. See WALSTAN.

BONIFACE

Boniface (Winfred) was a Benedictine monk, from Crediton in Devon. He despised opportunities of success in his own country and became a missionary in Frisia, where, however, his work was hampered by warfare and by the hostility of King Radbod. At the instigation of Pope Gregory II he extended his range and preached the Faith energetically, but with uneven success, throughout Hesse, Thuringia, and Bavaria. After another visit to Frisia, where he laboured with humility as assistant to St. Willibrord, Boniface went back, with matured powers and experience, to the district of Hesse. Consecrated bishop in 722 and later archbishop, he strove to establish order and discipline in the churches of France as well as Germany, but he had no fixed see until, in 745, Mainz was assigned to him. He displayed great zeal in the foundation of schools and monasteries, and was regarded as confidential adviser by King Pepin III. In 752 he gave up his position of authority and returned to unpretentious missionary work in the diocese of Utrecht, where he was murdered. The incident in the life of Boniface which caught the medieval imagination was his felling of the enormous oak-tree, sacred to Thor, at Fritzlar, but English artists do not seem to have copied those Continental craftsmen who portrayed him as wearing episcopal vestments and cutting down an oak.

BOTOLPH

Botolph, who is claimed by some as an Irishman, became abbot of 'Ikanhoe'—perhaps Iken, in Suffolk. He is said to have been an advocate of the full and careful observance by monasteries of the Benedictine Rule, at a time when it was not popular in England, about A.D. 640. His fame is attested by the dedication to him in East Anglia of some sixty-five churches, including that of Boston. He had no distinctive emblem, but appears as an abbot, sometimes holding a church.

BRENDAN

Brendan was an enterprising Irish missionary of the sixth century A.D. and reputed founder of many monasteries, including those of Clonfert and Annadown. Remarkable stories gathered round his name, the most famous being the account of his voyage for seven years amongst the enchanted islands of the eastern sea. The islands offered unalloyed and supernatural delights; but Brendan and his companions were sorely molested by demons whilst they sailed from place to place and at one point they met Judas enjoying a cheerless respite from the pangs of Hell as he sat alone on a desolate wind-swept rock. Two English churches, Brendon in Devonshire and Brancepeth in Durham, are dedicated to St. Brendan.

BRICE

As archdeacon to St. Martin, bishop of Tours (about A.D. 400), he often behaved in a troublesome and malicious manner. But, after his election to succeed Martin as bishop, he changed his ways and became notable for his devotion. He is occasionally depicted holding live coals in his garments. This refers to a test which he voluntarily undertook in order to refute those who slanderously imputed to him the parentage of an illegitimate child. But, in spite of the fact that neither Brice nor his clothing was harmed by the burning coals, he was ejected from his bishopric for seven years and thus purged the contempt which he had shown to St. Martin.

BRANWALLADER

Branwallader is said to have been a British prince who became 'a holy bishop'. His head was formerly preserved at Milton Abbas, Dorset, where the church is dedicated to several saints, of whom he is one.

BRIDGET OF KILDARE

Bridget, or Bride, of Kildare (about A.D. 452–523), one of the favourite saints of Ireland, has nineteen churches dedicated to her in England. She is represented as a nun, or abbess, holding a book but, in English churches, she receives no distinctive symbol drawn from the record of her impulsive generosity or the rapt spirituality which even caused her, in her heedlessness of material things, to hang her cloak on a sunbeam. Starting off, perhaps under the influence of St. Patrick, with a determination to live the life of a consecrated virgin in her own home, Bridget later felt constrained to preside over a small community of seven like-minded followers; then, as her fame increased and a vast crowd of disciples thronged her, she established a number of fair-sized convents of which the double monastery at Kildare was the most famous. Her nuns were required to pass their days in strict asceticism and devotion, varied by works of practical charity shown to the sick and poor and by careful study of the art of illuminating manuscripts.

Bridget of Kildare may sometimes be confused with another St. Bridget, a Swedish noblewoman who, after her husband's death (A.D. 1344), retired from the splendours of court life in order to devote herself to the practices of religion. She is honoured as the foundress of the Order of Brigittine nuns, and appears as a crowned abbess on the rood-screens at Kenn and Wolborough, Devon, and Westhall, Suffolk.

CALIXTUS

Calixtus (Callistus), pope of Rome 218–23. He is said to have been a slave who started a savings bank, which failed. When trying to extract some money owed to him by certain Jews he provoked a riot in a synagogue, and was condemned to work in the mines of Sardinia. His return, under an amnesty, scandalized Pope Victor, who persuaded him to withdraw to Antium, about forty miles distant from Rome, but he was welcomed back by the next pope, Zephyrinus, and appointed to control the Roman clergy and to supervise the cemeteries. Calixtus was bitterly assailed by St. Hippolytus, who charged him with unsoundness of doctrine and laxity in the administration of Church discipline; nevertheless, when Zephyrinus died, Calixtus rather than Hippolytus was chosen to succeed him. Calixtus is said to have met a martyr's death, being scourged and then flung out of a window into a pit by order of the emperor Alexander Severus. He is very rarely represented in English churches; at Wiggenhall St. Mary Magdalen, Norfolk, he appears as a pope wearing the tiara and holding a book and a long cross.

CANDIDA

Several martyrs of this name are commemorated in the Roman Calendar. The most famous Candida is said to have been put to death outside the gates of Rome during the persecution of Diocletian, about A.D. 303. She was not very celebrated in England, but at Whitchurch Canonicorum, Dorset, there is a dedication to 'St. Candida and the Holy Cross'.

Some would maintain that this 'Candida' is not the Roman martyr, but a local St. Wita whose body rests in a shrine in the north transept of the church.

CASSIAN

A Christian schoolmaster at Imola, in northern Italy, who defied the command of the emperor Diocletian and refused to sacrifice to pagan deities. He was abandoned to the tender mercies of his pupils, who stabbed him to death with their pens. Another Cassian was an Egyptian who crossed the sea to Marseilles and proceeded thence to Autun, where he was appointed bishop and occupied the see with distinction for twenty years (A.D. 377–97). The church of Chaddesley Corbett, Worcestershire, is dedicated to St. Cassian, but no local traditions remain to show which Cassian is thus honoured.

CATHARINE OF ALEXANDRIA

Catharine is perhaps rightly identified with the unnamed lady of Alexandria who, as the church historian Eusebius relates, withstood the tyrant Maximin (A.D. 307). Eusebius' story runs thus: 'A certain Christian lady, the most famous and distinguished of those at Alexandria, conquered the lustful and licentious spirit of Maximin by her remarkable courage and resolution. Renowned for wealth and birth and education, she yet had put everything second to modest conduct. Maximin found his advances again and again repulsed, but he was unable to put her to death (although she was quite ready to die) because his lust overcame his anger. So he punished her with exile and possessed himself of all her property.'[1] In medieval legend, illustrated by stained glass in a nave window at York Minster, this bare outline is filled in with picturesque detail. Catharine has become a royal personage, daughter of King Costus of Cyprus, and she appears before Maximin whose advances she rejects and whose chosen philosophers she overthrows in skilful argument. Maximin, enraged, orders the execution of the inept philosophers and causes Catharine to be bound to spiked wheels which

[1] *Ecclesiastical History*, viii. 14.

are, however, straightway shattered by angels. She is then beheaded and her body miraculously transferred to Mount Sinai. St. Catharine's usual emblem is her familiar wheel, but sometimes she holds a sword instead. She is the patron of learning, and of all teachers.

CATHARINE OF SIENA

Catharine of Siena (A.D. 1347–80), the twenty-fifth child of a wool-dyer, showed a precocious and extra-ordinary genius for religion. At the age of fifteen she took the habit of a Dominican tertiary and, while continuing to live in her own room, strove to imitate the life of the desert hermits. Her contemplation was rewarded with the most vivid intimations of spiritual reality which strengthened her to meet continuous ill health with cheerful confidence and to exert a redeem-ing influence over even the most hardened and wordly of those who met her. St. Catharine's reputation for insight was such that rulers in Church and State sought her advice. It was largely through her appeals that Pope Gregory XI was induced to return to Rome from Avignon and, when Urban VI was ad-vanced to the papacy in 1378, she was influential in securing support for him against the pretensions of the anti-pope who was elected by the seceding French cardinals. She spent the last two years of her life at Rome, and there counselled a reform of the Domini-can Order which was carried into effect. St. Catharine, who was canonized in 1461, lived too late to gain much popularity in England, but she is occasionally represented, as the type of the Christian mystic, wearing a crown of thorns and holding a burning heart in her hand.

CECILIA

Though a member of a noble Roman family, she was beheaded for her firm refusal to sacrifice to idols, in the third century A.D. Her legend makes her successful in converting to the Christian faith many persons, including her husband Valerian, with whom she lived in virginal wedlock. Cecilia is commonly distinguished by a garland, either of roses or of lilies, since two such garlands were said to have been brought for Valerian and herself from Paradise by an angel. Sometimes[1] she holds a harp or organ-pipes because, when she heard the organ making music for her wedding, she 'sang in her heart' to God, dedicating herself to Him alone. She is therefore patron saint of musicians.

[1] But apparently not in English pre-Reformation pictures.

CELESTINE

After being archdeacon of Rome he was elected pope in A.D. 422. He strove to enhance the privileges of his see and played a prominent part in combating the 'impiety and treason' of Nestorius, who appeared to deny the divinity of Christ. Celestine was at any rate partly responsible for the sending of Germanus and Lupus to Britain in A.D. 429 in order to refute Pelagian teaching about grace and free-will, and he also dispatched missionaries to Ireland. He is portrayed, but without any distinguishing emblem, in the east window of York Minster.

CHAD

A disciple of St. Aidan, and therefore representing Celtic rather than Roman Christianity, Chad became abbot of Lastingham in A.D. 664. He was promoted to the missionary bishopric of York but, finding himself opposed by Theodore, the new archbishop of Canterbury, and by St. Wilfrid, he went back to Lastingham. He was, however, held in such high regard for saintliness of life that he was summoned from his retirement to be bishop of Mercia (A.D. 670–2). Chad has no distinctive emblem. He appears as a bishop, sometimes holding a church because he established his see at Lichfield and is regarded as the founder of that cathedral.

CHARLES

The Book of Common Prayer, as revised in 1662, contained a 'Form of Prayer with Fasting to be used yearly upon the thirtieth of January, being the Day of the Martyrdom of the blessed King Charles I'. This commemoration, along with those of Gunpowder Treason and Charles II's Restoration, was abolished in 1859, but the royal martyr is honoured by five dedications, the oldest being that at Falmouth, where the church was consecrated in 1663.

CHRISTINA

Christina is an unsubstantial figure. Her legend makes her a maiden of noble birth who destroyed idols and was martyred in A.D. 287 at Bolsena in Tuscany. She survived attempts to burn and to drown her, and was eventually shot by arrows. Her emblem is therefore an arrow or, occasionally, a millstone.

CHRISTOPHER

Christopher was perhaps a martyr in Asia Minor during the persecution of Decius (A.D. 250). A church was dedicated to him at Constantinople as early as 452 and, in the Middle Ages, he enjoyed remarkable popularity. He was looked on as an intercessor powerful 'to put away sickness and sores from them that remember his passion and figure', as the *Golden Legend* has it, and nearly every parish church possessed a statue or a wall painting of St. Christopher, usually situated opposite the south door, to inspire daily devotion. For

If thou the face of Christopher on any morn shalt see
Throughout the day from sudden death thou shalt
    preserved be.[1]

Christopher was described as a giant who wished to serve the greatest king in the world. After several disappointments, he met a hermit who preached to him about Jesus Christ and suggested to him that he should take up his abode on the bank of a swift-running and dangerous river nearby and assist wayfarers to cross it. One day Christopher was carrying a child across when the waters rose alarmingly and

[1] Cristofori faciem die quacunque tueris
  Illa nempe die morte mala non morieris.
Several variants of the doggerel rhyme were current.

Christopher's burden seemed as heavy as the weight of the whole world. The reason for this became clear when the other bank was reached and the Child revealed Himself as Jesus Christ, Creator of the world.

Christopher subsequently met a martyr's death, but he is nearly always represented as a giant holding a great staff as he wades through the river, carrying the Christ-child on his shoulder. Sometimes the hermit is included in the picture—a diminutive figure standing on the far bank and holding a lantern.

CLARE

(A.D. 1194–1253.) Converted to a desire for poverty and asceticism by the influence of St. Francis of Assisi, she gave herself up to the monastic life and founded the order of the 'poor Clares'. Her exceptional charity and devotion won for her the solace of heavenly visions as well as the respect of her contemporaries, from Pope Innocent III down to the humblest citizen of Assisi. In English churches Clare is seldom depicted. When she does appear, as on a screen-panel at Trimingham, Norfolk, she is dressed as an abbess and holds a monstrance. This commemorates her success in repelling the Saracens of the emperor Frederick II from her nunnery by appearing before them, bearing a monstrance that contained the Blessed Sacrament.

CLEMENT

Bishop of Rome, about A.D. 90, and the reputed author of an extant letter that gives friendly warning and advice from the Roman church to the church of Corinth. His popularity in the Middle Ages was due to a tradition that he was sent into exile on the shores of the Black Sea where he was so successful in converting people to Christianity and overthrowing 'the temples of the idols' that the envoy of the emperor Trajan tied an anchor round his neck and drowned him. Thereafter every year, on the day of his martyrdom, the waters of the Black Sea miraculously parted to disclose a marble shrine in which his body lay. Clement therefore appears as a pope, with tiara and double or triple cross, holding an anchor.

COLUMBA

An energetic founder of monasteries and schools in Ireland, he became involved in civil strife and, in 563, sailed away to the island of Iona, off the coast of Argyllshire. Here the monastery was established from which the missionaries went out who proclaimed the Gospel in Scotland and Northumbria. Columba himself was pre-eminent for the tireless zeal of his evangelism, but he found time also to copy fine manuscripts, to write poetry, and to champion the Irish bards when they were threatened with expulsion from their country. He died in A.D. 597 at the age of seventy-six.

COLUMBAN

An Irish monk whose missionary zeal caused him to set out from Bangor (Co. Down) about A.D. 585, and travel through France, preaching and teaching. He eventually settled at Luxeuil, in Burgundy, and attracted many to his monasteries in spite of the severe rule of labour and discipline there imposed. Columban was tenacious in observing certain rites and customs of the Irish church, thus giving offence to the local clergy, and when, in addition, he earned the enmity of the court by fearless denunciations of laxity and vice, he was obliged to flee the country. After a troublous stay at Bregenz, he moved to Bobbio, in Lombardy, where he established a notable monastery and died in A.D. 615.

CONSTANTINE

Three churches in England are dedicated to St. Constantine. This is not the emperor Constantine who reversed the policy of his predecessors (A.D. 312) and, instead of repressing Christianity, established it as the official religion of the Roman empire. According to the chronicler Gildas, St. Constantine was a king of Cornwall in the sixth century A.D., whose way of life was in many respects deplorable. Chastened, however, by the death of his wife, he abandoned royal splendours and retired to a monastery in Ireland, where at first his position was that of a servant to the monks, and his chief duty to grind corn for them. But, his identity being discovered, he was permitted to devote himself to study and later became a missionary in Scotland under the direction of St. Columba, meeting a martyr's death in the wilds of Kintyre.

CORNELIUS

Pope of Rome, A.D. 251–3. During his short episcopate he was harassed by religious controversies, by the appearance of a rival pope, and by imperial persecutions, and he died in exile. Cornelius is represented as a pope, wearing the tiara and holding a horn (*cornu*). This allusion to his name is carried one degree farther in France, where he is the patron saint of oxen.

COSMAS AND DAMIAN

Two Arabian physicians of Aegae, in Cilicia, who were renowned for their skill in curing both men and animals and for their refusal to accept any fee in return for their services. Legend has it that they resolutely declined to sacrifice to idols and were therefore beheaded after torture in A.D. 287. Cosmas and Damian are not often depicted in English churches. When they appear, as at Wolborough in Devon, they hold a pestle and mortar or a glass phial or some other piece of medical equipment.

CRISPIN AND CRISPINIAN

Crispin and Crispinian are said in the *Golden Legend* to have been Romans who migrated to Soissons, where they gained renown both as skilful cobblers who usually declined any payment for their services and as persuasive preachers of Christianity. Because of their refusal to sacrifice to idols they were pierced with shoemaker's awls and suffered other tortures, being finally beheaded by order of the emperor Maximian, about A.D. 290.

CUTHBERT

Cuthbert was a Tweeddale shepherd who, influenced by a vision of angels bearing the soul of St. Aidan to heaven, joined the monastery of Melrose, whence he made frequent and arduous missionary journeys. In 664 he was chosen as prior of Lindisfarne but, though his life there was ordered by stern self-discipline, he felt impelled to still stricter asceticism as a hermit on one of the Farne Islands. He yielded to earnest entreaties and accepted the bishopric of Lindisfarne in 685, but retired, after two years of diligent pastoral activity, to his cell on Farne to die. The body of St. Cuthbert was eventually transferred to Durham in a coffin containing other relics, including the head of St. Oswald, and this association has caused Cuthbert to be sometimes represented holding King Oswald's head in his hands.

CUTHBURGA

A sister of Ina, king of Wessex, she married prince Aldfrid of Northumbria, but her husband permitted her to fulfil her heart's desire and lead a monastic life. She retired to the convent of Barking but was later invited by Ina to return to Wessex and organize a nunnery at Wimborne. Tradition is silent concerning the details of Cuthburga's life, but her ability and spiritual power are witnessed to by the reputation which her nunnery soon gained for learning and devotion. She died about 724, and is commemorated as the patron saint of Wimborne Minster.

CYPRIAN

Cyprian's virtues as scholar, administrator, and martyr received little attention in the Middle Ages. He was disregarded by the medieval artist and appears not to have been honoured by any church dedications except the now-demolished chapel of St. Cyprian-on-the-Sands, at Kirk Leatham, Yorkshire. Cyprian was a popular and distinguished lawyer at Carthage but, being converted to Christianity in A.D. 246, abandoned his secular career. He was ordained and his merits became so obvious that, two years later, he was promoted to be archbishop of Carthage, exercising authority over a large part of North Africa. He found much corruption and laxity to rebuke, but was soon faced with still greater troubles caused by the persecution of the emperor Decius. Cyprian withdrew from Carthage and, in answer to hostile critics, explained this action as prompted by a desire to continue the administration of the diocese and to lessen the danger of rioting. On his return, he was faced with difficult questions concerning the re-admission of those who, in time of stress, had denied the Faith, whilst his letters and the treatise 'On Unity' were influential in establishing Christian doctrine concerning baptism and the nature of the Church. But he never lost his pastoral enthusiasm and, on the outbreak of a severe epidemic of plague at Carthage, set an example of devotion in attending the sick without distinction of creed. When persecution was renewed, in 257, Cyprian was sent into exile, but the next year he was recalled and beheaded.

CYRIAC

Cyriac is said to have been a Roman deacon who, in spite of his success in expelling devils from the daughters both of the emperor Diocletian and of the king of Persia, suffered torture and execution for refusing to sacrifice to idols. Another Cyriac, more popularly venerated in England, was a three-year-old boy who, exclaiming 'I also am a Christian', ran towards his mother Julitta when she was about to be tortured as a condemned Christian, at Tarsus in Cilicia, about A.D. 300. Cyriac was seized by the governor and hurled down some steps, thus meeting his death at the same time as Julitta, who was beheaded.

DAVID

The most famous of the Welsh saints, he yet appears to have had no biography written until nearly five centuries after his death and the details of his career are uncertain. He is said to have excelled in the study of the scriptures and to have been founder and abbot of a monastery at the place in Pembrokeshire which now bears his name. Extreme asceticism and unremitting labour was the rule there, and, in order to secure them against the perils of idleness, the monks were yoked instead of oxen to the ploughs. Such was the impression made by his speeches at a council held to refute the Pelagian heresy that Dubricius, the archbishop of Wales, resigned and David was appointed by acclamation to succeed him. He showed great vigour in widespread missionary labours and in the establishment of new churches, and transferred his see from the Roman station of Caerleon-on-Usk to St. Davids, his settlement on the coast, whose remoteness favoured quiet contemplation and whence connexions with the Irish Church could easily be maintained. He died about A.D. 588.

DECUMAN

Decuman (Degeman) is said to have been a Welsh hermit who, in the seventh century, crossed to England and devoted himself there to a life of remote and solitary contemplation. A friendly cow visited him each day and provided him with the milk that was his main sustenance. He was eventually murdered at a point on the Somersetshire coast where the village of St. Decuman's now commemorates him.

DENIS (DIONYSIUS)

The apostle of France and first bishop of the region of Paris is identified, in some traditions, with Dionysius the Areopagite, one of St. Paul's Athenian converts. Other accounts delay his arrival at Paris until the middle of the third century. But all agree in describing his missionary zeal and the influence which he exercised over a hostile mob of pagans. He refused to carry out the state sacrifices enjoined by the civil power and was beheaded after torture. But 'anon the body of St. Denis raised himself up, and bare his head between his arms' and walked from Montmartre to his resting-place at St-Denis. He is therefore regularly represented as a bishop holding his mitred head in his hand.

DOMINIC

(A.D. 1170–1221.) Born of a noble Spanish family and becoming canon of Osma Cathedral in 1195, St. Dominic passed his early years in an austere but placid pursuit of learning and in the practice of self-denying charity. But discovering, in 1203, the lamentable state of the Christian Church in the south of France, he devoted himself to reforming the laxity of the Catholic Christians and to converting the Albigensian heretics. Round him gathered a small band of zealous missioners and, in 1218, Dominic received the sanction of Pope Honorius III for the establishment of his 'Order of Friars Preachers', who should travel far and wide proclaiming and expounding the true doctrine. The Black Friars reached England in 1221 and, by the time of the Reformation, had established some fifty-seven communities there. St. Dominic, though depicted on the Continent with a lily or a star as his emblems, failed to attract the attention of British artists.

DONATUS

The lives of two bishops, one of Euroea in Epirus and one of Arezzo in Tuscany, seem to have been confused in the *Golden Legend*. According to the account there given, Donatus was a pupil of the emperor Julian the Apostate. He fled to Arezzo and, becoming famous as a worker of miracles, was chosen to be bishop. In spite of his success in freeing a daughter of Theodosius I from diabolic possession, he met his death by beheading, about A.D. 380, for his refusal to 'do sacrifice to Jupiter'. Donatus may be represented as clad in armour, holding a crozier, and standing near a well. This refers to the story that Donatus prayed that an infected well might be purified, whereat a dragon rose up out of the water and attacked Donatus who struck the beast with his staff and killed it.

DOROTHY

A maiden of Caesarea in Cappadocia, she was renowned alike for her beauty and for her self-denying humility. At the time of the persecution ordered by the emperor Diocletian (about A.D. 300) she not only confessed herself to be a Christian but also rejected an offer of marriage from the prefect Fabricius. She suffered exemplary tortures with serenity, saying to the prefect: 'Do to me what torment thou wilt, for I am all ready to suffer it for the love of my spouse Jesu Christ, in whose garden full of delights I have gathered roses, spices and apples.' A scribe named Theophilus asked her, in jocular scorn, to grant him some of those roses and apples, and, after Dorothy had been beheaded, an angel appeared to Theophilus and presented him with a basket containing the roses and apples sent to him by Dorothy from Paradise, whereupon Theophilus was converted and received the crown of martyrdom. St. Dorothy is therefore shown holding flowers or fruit, usually in a basket.

DUBRITIUS (DEVEREUX)

The colourful but often conflicting traditions about St. Dubritius testify to the honour in which he was held but provide no very clear picture of his life and work. He is said to have been a Welshman of royal descent, founder of monasteries and monastic schools, who became bishop of Llandaff and was later promoted by King Arthur (!) to be archbishop of Caerleon. He resigned this dignity to St. David at the Council of Brefi (perhaps about A.D. 545) and spent his last days as a hermit on Bardsey Island. Several churches in Herefordshire, as well as that of Porlock, Somerset, are dedicated to St. Dubritius, but he passed unnoticed by medieval artists.

DUNSTAN

(A.D. 925–88.) As abbot of Glastonbury he enforced a strict observance of the Benedictine rules and
gained renown not only as scholar
and administrator but also for his
gifts as musician and goldsmith.
He was appointed chancellor to
King Edred but felt obliged to
rebuke the next king, Edwy, for
his immoralities, and was exiled
to Flanders. However, he was
recalled by King Edgar and
appointed bishop of Worcester
and, later, of London. After his
promotion, in 960, to the archbishopric of Canter-
bury, he enforced the strict discipline which his
monks at Glastonbury had felt upon all the clergy
and reformed the laxity of cathedral chapters. He
busied himself also with the details of civil administration and appears to have been at least partly
responsible for the beneficent reforms carried out by
Edgar; but, after the accession of King Ethelred, he
abandoned politics and devoted himself to the manifold cares of his diocese. When St. Dunstan bears a
distinguishing symbol, it is usually a pair of pincers.
This alludes to the occasion when, as he was busy
fashioning a chalice, the devil appeared, in the likeness of an attractive and wanton woman, to tempt
him with blandishments, whereat he seized his iron
tongs and gripped the devil by the nose.

EADBURGA

Several Saxon princesses remarkable for sanctity of life bore this name, which is a variant of Ethelburga, and at least two of them appear to be honoured by church dedications. The earlier, who may possibly have been the widow of Wulfhere, king of Mercia, is said to have received the veil at the hands of St. Egwin about A.D. 710 and to have become the second abbess of St. Peter's, Gloucester. Another Eadburga was the daughter of King Edward the Elder and lived in the tenth century. According to William of Malmesbury, she manifested her vocation to the monastic life when only three years old. The king devised the test of placing before her on one side a chalice and copy of the Gospels and, on the other side, some bracelets and necklaces; whereat the child, after sternly regarding the jewellery, stretched out her hands towards the chalice and book. This early choice was confirmed by her later inclinations. She lived in cheerful simplicity as a nun at Winchester and at Pershore, delighting to carry out such works of humble charity as washing socks for the other nuns while they slept.

EANSWITH

Daughter of King Eadbald of Kent, she declined an opportunity of becoming queen of Northumbria and preferred to found a nunnery at Folkestone, where she died perhaps about A.D. 650. Her emblem appears to be a fish, and she may be seen, on the seal of the corporation of Folkestone, standing, crowned and holding a crozier, between two fishes.

EATA

A pupil of St. Aidan, he was appointed abbot of Melrose about A.D. 650 and thus exercised influence over St. Cuthbert. He later became abbot of Lindisfarne as well, an irregularity which was justified by his gentleness and simple piety to which Bede testifies. For some years he was bishop of Lindisfarne but, in 685, he transferred to Hexham in favour of Cuthbert who strongly desired to have his see at Lindisfarne. The church at Atcham, Shropshire, is dedicated to St. Eata, and he appears on a screen-panel at Hexham as a bishop without distinctive symbol.

EBBE

Ebbe, or Ebba, was a daughter of Ethelfrid, king of Northumbria, and, under the patronage of her brother, King Oswy, she founded a nunnery at Ebchester, on the Derwent. She later became abbess of a 'double' monastery, containing both monks and nuns, at Coldingham (St. Abbe's Head) on the coast of Berwickshire, where St. Cuthbert used to visit her to offer prayer and counsel. But her last years were clouded owing to indiscipline and laxity in her monastery, which was burned to the ground shortly after her death in A.D. 683. St. Ebbe was acclaimed as a miracle-worker, and churches are dedicated to her at Oxford, where she is shown, in restored fifteenth-century glass, with pastoral staff and book, and at Ebchester.

EDITH

Some twenty churches are dedicated to St. Edith, and it is not possible in every case to determine whether St. Edith of Polesworth or St. Edith of Wilton is intended to be patron. Edith of Polesworth is said to have been a daughter of King Edward the Elder. Political expediency rather than affection caused her to marry Sithric the Dane, but, on her husband's death a year later, she retired to live a life of devotion at Polesworth, in Warwickshire, and became abbess there. Edith of Wilton was the daughter of King Edgar and of the nun Wolfrida. She was taken by her mother to Wilton abbey and educated there, and, becoming known for her gentle manners and unassuming piety, was, at the king's request, elected abbess of Barking. But she refused this dignity and remained at Wilton, where she died at the age of twenty-three (A.D. 984).

EDMUND

Edmund was king of East Anglia from 855 until he died (870). During his reign the Danes, led by Inguar and Ubba, began to harass his land. Edmund was defeated in battle and taken prisoner, but he declined to parley with the Danes or renounce his faith, wherefore, after being submitted to Inguar's taunts, he was tied to a tree, shot with arrows, and finally beheaded. The king's death is traditionally connected with the village of Hoxne in Suffolk, and, until its fall in 1848, an ancient oak was pointed out as the tree to which Edmund was bound; but other accounts mention Sutton, near Woodbridge, as the scene of his martyrdom. The story is told that the Danes threw the king's head into the undergrowth of a thick wood, so that it might corrupt in dishonour, but it was discovered through its ability to cry out 'Here, here' when it was being sought for. It had been preserved from the wild beasts by a huge grey wolf, which accompanied the funeral cortège to Bury St. Edmund's and then quietly returned to the wood. The popularity of St. Edmund is attested by some sixty dedications and by his frequent appearance on the screen-panels of East Anglian churches. His usual emblem is an arrow, or handful of arrows, but representations of the wolf guarding the king's head are occasionally to be seen.

EDMUND OF ABINGDON

Edmund of Abingdon (*c.* 1175–1240) was austerely brought up by his mother, Mabel Rich. He spent long periods of study at Paris and at Oxford, where he placed a ring upon the finger of a statue of the Virgin Mary and vowed that he would take no one else as his wife. He acquired a wide range of learning but, as the result of a vision, concentrated his attention on divinity, 'and when he read divinity in schools, his scholars and hearers profited more in one day than they did of other men's teaching a whole week'.[1] He was famous for the eloquence of his sermons and for his zeal in supporting the Crusades. One day, when he was preaching in the churchyard of All Hallows, Oxford, a dark rain-cloud approached. The people who ran away to shelter were drenched, but those who remained in the churchyard, listening to the sermon, were not touched by a drop of rain. Edmund Rich was appointed canon of Salisbury in 1222 and was advanced to the archbishopric of Canterbury in 1233. In this office he showed himself charitable to the poor but unyielding in his defence of the privileges of the Church, and, after bitter controversies with King Henry III, he retired to the abbey of Pontigny, where he died. He is patron of St. Edmund Hall, Oxford.

[1] *Golden Legend.*

EDWARD THE CONFESSOR

 The last of the Anglo-Saxon kings had little taste for statecraft, and his reign (A.D. 1042–66) was not marked by quite such unalloyed joy and prosperity as were sometimes claimed for it by the old chroniclers. But Edward was notable for his meekness and piety, for the gift of prophetic second-sight which caused him to forecast grievous disasters that would afflict England after his death, for his power to heal the sick or the blind, and for the devotion which led him to refound Westminster Abbey in enhanced splendour. He was present at the dedication of the church at Havering, in Essex, to the honour of Christ and St. John the Evangelist, and, in the course of the ceremony, an old man asked alms of him. The king had no money to offer but took the ring from his finger and gave that to the beggar, who thanked him and departed. Years later the same old man appeared to certain English pilgrims in Palestine and handed them the ring, explaining that he was John the Evangelist who had been present at the dedication of his church and that he now wished to return the ring and to inform King Edward that within six months he would die and attain to the joys of Heaven. St. Edward the Confessor is therefore usually depicted holding a ring.

EDWARD THE MARTYR

Edward the Martyr succeeded his father Edgar as king of Wessex but incurred the enmity of his step-mother who coveted the throne for her own son Ethelred. She was residing at Corfe Castle when Edward, who was out hunting, called to visit her. Food and wine were offered to him, but, while he was drinking, the queen's brother struck him through with a dagger (A.D. 979). His body, which proved to be endowed with miraculous powers of healing disease, was taken to Wareham and then transferred with great solemnity to the convent at Shaftesbury. From the manner of his death, St. Edward the Martyr is shown as a king holding a cup or a dagger.

EDWIN

Edwin (585–633), a warlike and ambitious king of Northumbria, married, in 625, Ethelburga, sister of Eadbald the Christian king of Kent. Eadbald made it a condition of the engagement that Ethelburga should be free to practise her religion, and Paulinus accompanied her to Northumbria in the role of a courtier-bishop. Pope Boniface V sent Edwin a letter, accompanied by some valuable robes, begging him to heed the teaching of Paulinus, and, gratified by an unexpected victory over the West Saxons, Edwin consented to receive instruction in the Christian faith. He proved a somewhat arrogant pupil, but Paulinus played skilfully on his hopes and fears until he accepted baptism at York in 627 and persuaded many members of the Witan to follow his example. Edwin's conversion was sincere, he became a zealous patron of Paulinus and ruled his kingdom with such justice and charity that it was claimed that 'a woman with a new-born infant might walk from one end of Edwin's land to another and no one would do her harm'. But he had a taste for power and splendour which provoked the jealousy of Penda, king of Mercia, and, when the two armies met at Heathfield, near Doncaster, Edwin was slain and his troops routed. Edinburgh is said to be named after him, and he has a church dedication at Coniscliffe, Durham.

EDWOULD

A late and uncertain tradition[1] makes Edwould a brother of St. Edmund, king of the East Angles, and relates that, after Edmund's untimely death, Edwould, despising the vanities of this world, retired to pass his days in simple asceticism as a hermit at Cerne, Dorset. The church of Stockwood, not far from Cerne, commemorates this royal anchorite in its dedication.

[1] In William of Malmesbury's *Gesta Pontificum*.

EGWIN

His somewhat dubious biographies record that Egwin, bishop of Worcester about A.D. 694–710, was a member of the royal house of Mercia who was appointed to the see of Worcester with the enthusiastic approval of everyone except himself. But he showed such zeal in the discharge of his pastoral office that he was accused of undue strictness and decided to go on a penitential pilgrimage to Rome in order to clear himself. He fixed iron fetters about his feet and threw into the River Avon the key which locked them, but, on the arrival of his ship at Rome, he was presented with a fish which proved to contain the key, so Egwin removed his fetters and, fully vindicated by the Pope, returned to the administration of his diocese. He was active as a church builder and established the famous monastery of Evesham.

ELEUTHERUS

A Greek who became deacon to Pope Anicetus and was himself pope from A.D. 174 to 189. Little is known of his pontificate beyond the fact that he had to guard the faith of the Church against the acute but dangerous speculations of heretical teachers. Bede, in his *Ecclesiastical History*,[1] relates that a certain 'King Lucius of Britain' appealed to Eleutherus to send missionaries to convert the British people, a task which they successfully accomplished. This story, which received enthusiastic embellishments from such chroniclers as Geoffrey of Monmouth, appears to lack any foundation of fact, but in two of the windows of York Minster Lucius and Eleutherus are portrayed standing near one another.

[1] i. 4.

ELIZABETH

The incident in the life of the mother of John the Baptist which appealed to the medieval artist is taken from St. Luke's Gospel (i. 39–45) where, in answer to the salutation of her cousin, the Virgin Mary, she replied, with prophetic insight, 'Blessed art thou among women and blessed is the fruit of thy womb'. Apocryphal tradition had stories to tell of her flight to the hill country in order to protect her son from Herod's slaughter of the children of Bethlehem.

ELIZABETH OF HUNGARY

(A.D. 1207–31.) A daughter of King Andrew II of Hungary, she married Louis, landgrave of Thuringia, and bore him three children. But she derived no pleasure from the splendours of her position and, in spite of taunts and reproaches which she had to endure on account of her desire for strict simplicity of life, devoted much of her time to prayer and works of charity. Her husband died in 1227 while on his way to take part in a Crusade. Thereafter, under the austere guidance of her spiritual director, Conrad of Marburg, she adopted a life of strict asceticism and poverty, rejoicing in the performance of the humblest duties while nursing the sick in a hospital founded by herself. 'She had a special grace to weep abundantly tears, for to see celestial visions, and for to inflame the hearts of others to the love of God.'[1] When St. Elizabeth of Hungary is represented in English churches she wears a crown and holds a cup and loaves or a rose. The latter emblem refers to an occasion when, as she was taking food to the poor in a large basket, she was stopped by her husband who had become irritated by what he regarded as her wasteful habits. But, when the basket was opened, all that the landgrave saw was a mass of red roses.

[1] *Golden Legend.*

ELOY (ELIGIUS)

According to his *Life*, Eloy or Eligius was a gold-smith of Limoges who migrated and found favour at the court of Clotaire II and, later, Dagobert I, kings of the Franks. He bestowed all his money to aid the poor and gained such repute for self-sacrificing piety that he was chosen bishop of Noyon (A.D. 640). His diocese extended into Flanders, where he devoted himself to missionary endeavour and to such charit-able actions as the burial of executed criminals. St. Eloy is represented as a bishop holding a hammer or a horseshoe and, occasionally, a horse's leg as well. This recalls the story that he once cut off a horse's leg, shod the hoof, and replaced the leg—a feat which caused St. Eloy to become patron saint of farriers.

ERASMUS

Erasmus (Elmo) is said to have been 'bishop of Campania' (central Italy). He survived savage tortures in the persecution of Diocletian and then, refusing to give up his vigorous preaching of the Christian faith, was put to death by order of the emperor Maximian, about A.D. 303. The most notable of his torments was the attempt to draw the entrails out of his body by means of a windlass, and the windlass thus became the regular emblem of St. Erasmus, who was widely venerated in the Middle Ages and invoked by those who wished to avoid intestinal troubles or seasickness. (*See* p. xxxvii)

ERKENWALD

Erkenwald, a member of the royal family of East Anglia, founded two monasteries, one for men, at Chertsey, of which he became abbot, and another for women, at Barking, which he entrusted to the care of his sister, Ethelburga. In 676 he was consecrated by Theodore of Canterbury as bishop of London and, though the details of his episcopate are obscure, the enthusiastic praise for sanctity of life that is accorded to him by Bede[1] indicates that he was a man well qualified to direct an important diocese during its transition from the missionary stage to the period of settled organization. Erkenwald was honoured as the founder of St. Paul's Cathedral and his body was laid to rest there in a wonder-working shrine, despite the claims of Chertsey and Barking to so valuable a relic. When St. Erkenwald is depicted, as at Guilden Morden, Cambridgeshire, he appears in the vestments of a bishop but lacks any distinctive emblem.

[1] *Ecclesiastical History*, iv. 6.

ETHELBERT

The saint to whom Hereford Cathedral and some fourteen other churches are dedicated is not the king of Kent who was converted by St. Augustine's mission in A.D. 597, but a king of East Anglia who was beheaded by Offa of Mercia in A.D. 794. The story, as elaborated by such chroniclers as William of Malmesbury, runs that Ethelbert, who had gained the affection of his subjects by his prudence and piety, set off from Bury St. Edmund's, in spite of such adverse portents as an earthquake and an eclipse, to seek the hand of Offa's daughter in marriage. His suit prospered only too well, in that Offa's wife, Queen Cynethritha, hearing her daughter speak of Ethelbert in terms of extravagant praise, was filled with jealousy and persuaded Offa that Ethelbert should be seized and beheaded. The king's body was conveyed to Hereford, where his shrine became notable as the scene of miraculous healings. St. Ethelbert has no fixed emblem but, in fourteenth-century glass at Hereford Cathedral, he holds a sword and a church.

ETHELBURGA

Several Anglo-Saxon queens and abbesses bore this name, and the distinction between them cannot always be drawn with certainty. Two Ethelburgas appear to have been honoured with church dedications. One was a sister of Erkenwald, bishop of London, who appointed her the first abbess of a convent which he founded at Barking, about A.D. 665. Here she gained repute for sanctity of life and as the recipient of prophetic visions.

The other was the daughter of Ethelbert, king of Kent, who consented to be betrothed to Edwin, king of Northumbria, only on condition that he showed no hostility to the Christian religion and would himself accept it if, on examination, it proved superior to his ancestral cult. Edwin was soon converted, but died in battle in A.D. 633. Ethelburga then returned to Kent, and tradition makes her the foundress of an abbey at Lyminge.

ETHELDREDA (AUDRY)

Daughter of Anna, king of East Anglia, she was married first to Prince Tondbert, who bestowed the Isle of Ely on her as dowry, and next to Egfrid, prince, and later king, of Northumbria. With the support of Wilfrid, archbishop of York, she left Egfrid, about A.D. 670, and fulfilled her true ambition by becoming a nun.

After a year in the convent at Coldingham, she came back to Ely, restored the church that had recently been destroyed by the pagan King Penda of Mercia, and established a nunnery of which Wilfrid appointed her the first abbess. She became renowned for strict asceticism and devotion, and her influence in life, as well as the presence of her uncorrupt and miracle-working body after death, turned Ely, then a remote island standing out amidst trackless swamps, into the most famous religious centre in East Anglia. St. Etheldreda is represented as a crowned abbess, with no characteristic emblem.

ETHELWALD (ADELWOLD)

A monk of Ripon, he took possession of the hermitage which St. Cuthbert had occupied on Farne Island and passed his days there in solitary contemplation. According to Bede, his prayers were effective in calming a storm which threatened to engulf three monks of Lindisfarne who were sailing home after visiting him. The church of Alvingham, Lincolnshire, is dedicated to St. 'Adelwold', possibly because some of his relics were bestowed upon a priory that was founded there in the twelfth century.

EUGENIA

Eugenia is shown in a wall-painting at Farnborough, Hampshire, but apparently occurs nowhere else in England. She seems to be an authentic virgin-martyr who suffered at Rome in the third century A.D., but the details of her life are unknown. The *Golden Legend* tells about her a story which, with slight variations, had become attached to several other names also. Eugenia is there described as the daughter of 'Philip, duke of Alexandria'. Arraying herself in man's clothing, she gained admittance to an Egyptian monastery and, because of her outstanding piety, was in due course chosen as abbot. A spiteful accusation of adultery caused her to be brought before her father for judgement, but she easily cleared herself of the charge by making her sex and identity known to him, with the result that he was converted to Christianity and later became a bishop and martyr.

EUPHEMIA

Euphemia is very rarely shown in English churches; indeed no certain representation of her is earlier than the seventeenth-century glass at Magdalen College, Oxford. She was a virgin-martyr who met her death at Chalcedon, a suburb of Constantinople, towards the end of the third century. The General Council of A.D. 451 met in the church dedicated to her at Chalcedon, and her relics were held in high honour at Constantinople until the emperor Constantine Copronymus threw them into the sea, but, though the antiquity of her cult is established, little is known about her life. Early traditions had it that she was arrested for refusing to join in pagan worship and, after surviving savage tortures, was executed by the sword, since the wild beasts to whom she was thrown fawned on her instead of mauling her.

EUSTACE

Eustace was, from very ancient times, commemorated at Rome as a martyr who had suffered, together with his wife Theopistis and his two sons, under the emperor Hadrian, about A.D. 120. His *Acts* add romantic details and relate that Eustace was Trajan's master of the horse and that, while out hunting, he was converted by the sight of a luminous cross and image of Christ set between the horns of a stag which he was pursuing. After he and his wife had been baptized, he was warned that he would suffer trials as grievous as those of Job. Loss of his possessions by theft and pestilence caused him to flee away to Egypt where his wife was retained by the captain of the ship, in lieu of the proper fare which Eustace was unable to pay. His sons were carried off, one by a lion and the other by a wolf, and he spent fifteen years, in tribulation and poverty, as a farm-labourer. Then, however, his fortune changed. He was sought out by messengers from the emperor Hadrian and recalled to take office again as master of the horse. His sons, who had been rescued by some ploughmen from the wild beasts, were discovered in the army under his command and his wife also was restored to him. But all four met their death for refusal to sacrifice to idols, being roasted in a brazen bull by Hadrian's command. A stag with a crucifix between

its horns is the emblem of St. Eustace, as it is also of St. Hubert, about whom a similar story was told of a vision in the hunting field. On the west front of Wells Cathedral, St. Eustace is shown carrying his two sons across a river.

EVERILDA

Her history and even her existence are uncertain.
She is said to have been converted by St. Birinus and
to have journeyed northwards, some years later, to
consult St. Wilfrid of York about the proper method
of devoting herself and two companions to the
monastic life. Wilfrid gave them a site on which to
build a nunnery, perhaps at Everingham, Yorkshire,
where the church is dedicated to St. Everilda.

EVURTIUS

Evurtius is probably to be identified with a bishop of
Orléans who was present at a Council of Valence in
A.D. 374. His *Acts* recount a string of fantastic
miracles, but are historically worthless. St. Evurtius
gained no popularity in England as a patron, but his
name, misspelt Enurchus, has appeared, since 1604,
in the Anglican calendar (7th September).

FABIAN

Pope of Rome A.D. 236–50. According to the historian Eusebius[1] he was, while still a layman, chosen pope by popular acclamation because a dove settled on his head. St. Cyprian of Carthage testifies to the excellence of his rule. He is thought to have divided Rome into seven spheres of administration, each under the control of a deacon, and to have embellished the cemeteries of Rome with new buildings. He was beheaded in the persecution enjoined by the emperor Decius.

[1] *Ecclesiastical History*, vi. 29.

FAITH

Faith suffered martyrdom at Agen, in Aquitaine, towards the end of the third century A.D. Her apocryphal legend records that she was stretched on a brass bedstead and roasted, and she therefore receives a metal bedstead or a gridiron as her emblem. But occasionally she holds a saw instead.

FELICIANUS

A rhetorician who was appointed bishop of Foligno by Pope Victor about A.D. 197. During the persecution set on foot by the emperor Decius in A.D. 250, Felicianus, then an extremely old man, was arrested and taken off in a cart to Rome, but he died on the way and is therefore reckoned as a martyr. St. Felicianus is very rarely to be seen in English churches. At Wiggenhall St. Mary Magdalen, Norfolk, he appears as a bishop without distinctive emblem.

·FELIX

Many saints and bishops bore this name, but the one to whom several English churches are dedicated and who occasionally appears in medieval stained glass, as at Blythburgh in Suffolk, is the Burgundian who was sent by Honorius, archbishop of Canterbury, to preach the Gospel in East Anglia and became the first bishop of Dunwich (about A.D. 630). Felix enjoyed the support of King Sigebert and later of King Anna, and, in spite of the hostile forays of the pagans of Mercia, was active and successful both as a missionary and as a founder of schools.

FINAN

Finan, a monk of Iona, succeeded Aidan as bishop of Lindisfarne in A.D. 652. He was an energetic missionary and church builder, and he helped the expansion of Christianity beyond the borders of Northumbria by baptizing Prince Peada of Mercia and King Sigebert of the East Saxons whose conversion had been effected by King Oswy. Bede, in his *Ecclesiastical History*,[1] describes Finan as a 'professed opposer of the truth' and 'a man of violent temper', but this condemnation seems to be due merely to the fact that Finan was inflexible in preferring the Celtic to the Roman method of observing Easter. St. Finan is rarely portrayed in English churches, and when he appears, as in a window of the choir at York Minster, he has no distinctive emblem.

[1] iii. 25.

FIRMIN

A Spanish convert who was ordained at Toulouse as a missionary bishop. He worked his way through Gaul to Amiens where, according to his *Acts*, he was beheaded by order of the Roman governor, at the end of the third century A.D. Two English churches, North Crawley and Thurlby, are dedicated to him.

FLORENCE

Florence is portrayed on a screen-panel at Ufford, Suffolk, but apparently nowhere else in England. She was a Phrygian maiden who received baptism at the hands of St. Hilary of Poitiers and, following him when he returned to Gaul, devoted herself to a solitary life of prayer and contemplation in Poitou. Another St. Florence, perhaps the one whom the artist at Ufford intended to represent, suffered martyrdom at Agde, in southern France, early in the fourth century.

FRANCIS

The founder of the Grey Friars was born at Assisi in
1182. After a normal boyhood he entered his father's
business and became a cloth-merchant, but sickness
and his experiences as a prisoner-of-war changed his
outlook and, to his father's extreme irritation, he
decided to devote himself in poverty to prayer and
works of charity. His mission-preaching attracted a
number of followers for whom he prepared a simple
rule which received the approval of Pope Innocent
III in 1210 and was revised, to suit the needs of a
rapidly increasing body of disciples, in 1223. The
miraculous healings performed by St. Francis, his
insight into the hearts of men, and his sympathy with
all creation were celebrated everywhere, but he is not
often represented in English churches. He may, however, appear as a friar holding a cross and occasionally he displays the marks which he received in hands,
feet, and side as the result of a vision of the crucified
Christ.

FRIDBERT

Fridbert succeeded St. Acca as bishop of Hexham in
A.D. 733. It is recorded that he took charge of the
see of Lindisfarne for one year when Bishop Cyne-
wulf was imprisoned for displeasing King Edbert,
but, beyond that, no traditions concerning his episcopate are preserved. He died in 766 and was buried
at Hexham, where he is depicted, on a panel of the
vestry screen, as a bishop without distinctive emblem.

FRIDESWIDE

Her legend, which is not found in fully developed
form until the fourteenth century, makes her a royal
maiden who refused an offer of marriage from Prince
Algar of Mercia and retired to live a life of contemplation at Binsey, near Oxford. When her suitor
persisted in trying to approach her, he was smitten
with blindness. Frideswide founded and became
abbess of a nunnery at Oxford, about A.D. 730, but
continued to spend much of her time in solitude at
Binsey. Soon after the solemn translation of her
relics, in 1180, to the abbey church, now the Cathedral, she was regarded as patron of the city and
University of Oxford, and her shrine became a place
of pilgrimage for both townsfolk and students.

FURSEY

Fursey was an Irishman of noble birth who founded
a monastery at Killursa, on the east side of Lough
Corrib. From time to time he fell into ecstasies and
saw visions of Heaven and Hell which were influential in fixing the medieval picture of the state of the
departed. About A.D. 633 Fursey migrated to East
Anglia and, under the patronage of King Sigebert,
settled at Burgh Castle, near Yarmouth. His mission-
preaching proved successful, but the disturbances
caused by the forays of King Penda of Mercia induced him to seek refuge in Gaul, where he founded
the monastery of Lagny as well as a number of
churches. He died about A.D. 650 and was buried at
Péronne.

GABRIEL

Gabriel, the archangel who 'stands in the presence of God'[1], owed his popularity in the Middle Ages to the part that he had played as the messenger sent to announce to the Virgin Mary her high destiny as mother of the Saviour.[2] Five or six English churches are dedicated to him, but he is chiefly honoured by the dedication of bells, since a special bell was rung daily to remind the faithful of their duty to repeat the salutation which Gabriel had addressed to the Virgin. He is variously represented in pictures of the Annunciation. He may stand or kneel before the Virgin or, less commonly, hover overhead. Sometimes his body is covered with scales and he wears a coronet; elsewhere he is shown clad in white and holding a lily, the emblem of purity. When he appears by himself, he usually bears a shield with Ave Maria engraved on it.

[1] St. Luke i. 19.   [2] Ibid. 26–38.

GENESIUS

Several saints bear this name, and their stories are apt
to be confused. One Genesius, a notary of Arles, was
required to read out in court an edict of the emperor
Diocletian authorizing the persecution of Christians.
Refusing to do so he fled from the city, but returned
in order to be baptized. Before this ceremony could
be carried out, soldiers arrived to arrest him, so he
plunged into the river Rhone and, on reaching the
other side, was seized, beheaded, and thus 'baptized
in his own blood'. Another Genesius, who also
suffered martyrdom about A.D. 303, was a comic
actor who, whilst ridiculing the rite of baptism, experienced a sudden conversion and, after testifying
to his Christianity, was beheaded. A figure on a
bench end at Combe-in-Teignhead, Devon, is sometimes said to represent St. Genesius the actor, but the
identification is very dubious. A third Genesius,
perhaps more firmly rooted in history, was, much
against his will, elected bishop of Clermont in A.D.
656. However, he grew tired of episcopal pomp and,
to the embarrassment of his flock, set out on a secret
pilgrimage to Rome. He was persuaded to return,
but died the following year, not before he had
founded the monastery of Manlieu.

GENEVIÈVE

Geneviève is the patron saint of Paris. Her *Legend*, which claims to have been written shortly after her death but which is romantic rather than historical, records that she was a maiden of Nanterre who, encouraged by St. German, resolved to devote herself, as the 'spouse of Christ', to a life of poverty and charitable works. Thereupon miraculous powers of healing and insight into men's minds were granted to her. She was protected alike from the irritation of her mother, who suffered temporary blindness for slapping her, from the envy of the citizens, and from the savagery of Attila and his Huns, who were diverted by her prayers from attacking Paris (A.D. 451). Her austerity was extreme and, until she reached the age of fifty, she was satisfied with a meal of bread and beans twice a week. By reason of her constant encouragement and her miraculous discovery of lime needed for the building, a church was constructed to the honour of St. Denis and his companions, and in it she rejoiced to spend hours of prayer and vigil. St. Geneviève was not a favourite saint in England, but she is occasionally depicted with a spinning-wheel, from a tradition which grew up that she was a shepherdess. Elsewhere, as on a screen-panel at Kenn, Devonshire, she holds a candle because she was enabled, by her prayers, to light a candle 'without any fire of this world' and to keep it burning even in a night of wind and rain.

GEORGE

The historian Gibbon took a perverse pleasure in identifying St. George with an energetic and unscrupulous pork-contractor, George of Cappadocia, who was for a time (A.D. 356–61) the Arian bishop of Alexandria. But St. George, though the details of his career are obscure, had probably lived some fifty years earlier, and churches seem to have been dedicated to him by the middle of the fourth century. Tradition claims that he was a soldier of Lydda, in Palestine, who met a martyr's death during the reign of Diocletian, and he has been, somewhat precariously, identified with the unnamed Christian who, as Eusebius[1] records, tore down the edict of persecution published at Nicomedia by order of that emperor in A.D. 303.

The *Golden Legend* has a sensational story to tell about him. He is there said to have saved the life of a princess who was about to be handed over as a propitiatory offering to a dragon which was plaguing her city. As the princess was being led, in bridal array, to the sacrifice, St. George arrived and, protected by the sign of the cross, disabled the dragon with a spear-thrust. The dragon was then led back to the city 'as it had been a meek beast and debonair' and its head was cut off, whereupon fifteen thousand

<hr />

[1] *Ecclesiastical History*, viii. 5.

men thankfully hastened to be baptized. Shortly afterwards St. George endured savage tortures and was put to death for resolutely declining to sacrifice to idols. St. George became patron saint of England as a result of the Crusades. He was popularly invoked by the Christian soldiers before battle was joined with the Saracens and, in particular, Richard Cœur de Lion had a vision assuring him of the saint's protection. But he did not finally supersede St. Edward the Confessor until King Edward III, while campaigning against the French, had proved the efficacy of the battle-cry 'St. George for England'. The medieval artists represented St. George as clad in armour and either piercing the dragon with his lance or slashing at it with a sword.

GERMAN

German, of Auxerre in the district of Lyons, was a
barrister of noble birth who was appointed duke of
Burgundy. He was devoted to the chase, and used
to hang the spoils of his hunting on a tree that stood
in the middle of Auxerre. The bishop, Amator, re-
proved him for this ostentation and eventually cut
down the tree, whereat German flew into a rage and
went with his knights to slay the bishop. But
Amator enticed him, unarmed, into the church and
forcibly ordained him. On Amator's death a few
days later German was unanimously acclaimed as
bishop and immediately changed his way of life,
bestowing his riches upon the poor and practising so
severe a discipline that, in the words of his biographer, he 'endured a prolonged martyrdom'. In
answer to an appeal by the clergy of Britain who were
vexed by the unorthodox views of the Pelagians concerning grace, freewill, and baptism, St. German and
St. Lupus of Troyes were sent to confute the heretics,
and successfully accomplished this task by triumph-
ing over the Pelagians in a public debate held near
St. Albans, about A.D. 430. They later helped the
British army to repel the Picts and Saxons by instructing the soldiers to raise the Easter cry 'Alleluia'
three times as their enemy approached. This was
done, and the invaders retreated in terror. German
was again summoned to Britain, in A.D. 447, to oppose
the Pelagians, and was honourably received by Galla
Placidia, mother of the emperor Valentinian III,
when he went to Ravenna to plead for the people of
Brittany, who had been guilty of revolt, but he did

not allow such ambassadorial journeys to deflect him from his works of penitence and humble charity. A dozen ancient churches in England are dedicated to St. German, but he is rarely depicted and then only as a bishop without characteristic emblem.

GERTRUDE

Gertrude (about A.D. 620–59), daughter of Pepin of Landen, mayor of the palace to the Frankish King Dagobert I, refused all offers of marriage and retired with her mother, St. Iduberga, to a double monastery which Iduberga had established at Nivelles, in Brabant. Gertrude was appointed abbess, and soon gained a reputation for piety, hospitality to visitors, and deep learning in the scriptures. She also encouraged the Irish monks, Foillan and Ultan, to settle in the neighbourhood and provide a hospice for strangers. After her mother's death she found administrative cares increasingly burdensome and resigned the office of abbess, devoting the last three years of her life to prayer and rigid asceticism. On the Continent St. Gertrude was a popular patron saint of travellers and was invoked to ward off rats and mice: she is occasionally shown in English churches as an abbess writing in a book, or with mice on her crozier. The original reason for her mice seems merely to be that her feast-day, 17 March, occurs about the time when field mice emerge from their hibernation and become a nuisance.

GERVASIUS AND PROTASIUS

Gervasius and Protasius are revered as the first martyrs of Milan. When, in A.D. 386, St. Ambrose was about to dedicate his new church—the predecessor of the present S. Ambrogio—his heart 'burned within him as with a kind of presentiment'[1] and he caused excavations to be made in a neighbouring cemetery. Two large skeletons were discovered, identified with St. Gervasius and St. Protasius, and, amid great popular enthusiasm, transferred by Ambrose to his new church. A blind man, some demoniacs, and other sick persons were healed by touching or even by approaching the bier, and the two martyrs were acclaimed as the defenders and champions of Milan. Of Gervasius and Protasius nothing certain was remembered except that they had been put to death in Nero's time. But a tradition soon crystallized that they were sons of another martyr, named Vitalis, and that, after the death of their parents, they sold their property for the benefit of the poor and lived a monastic life for ten years, but, refusing to join in pagan sacrifices on behalf of a military expedition which was setting out against the German tribes, were seized and summarily executed. They gained no great repute in England as patrons, but the church at Little Plumstead, Norfolk, is dedicated to them.

[1] Ambrose, Letter 22.

GILDARD

It was thought, in the Middle Ages, that St. Gildard, bishop of Rouen, and St. Medard were twin brothers who died on the same day, but Gildard seems, in fact, to have been older than Medard and to have been promoted to the see of Rouen before A.D. 510. He is very rarely to be seen in English churches, but a fifteenth-century window at Wiggenhall, Norfolk, shows him standing next to St. Medard and holding book and crozier.

GILES

Giles was a most popular patron, to whom nearly a hundred and fifty churches are dedicated in England, but the details of his life are unknown. His late and untrustworthy *Acts* record that he travelled from Greece to Gaul, towards the end of the seventh century A.D., and then, wishing to avoid the notoriety which his miraculous powers threatened to cause, withdrew to live as a hermit in a remote forest. A hind dwelt with him in his cave and supplied him with milk. One day this hind was pursued  by the king's huntsmen and fled for succour to St. Giles whose prayers repelled the hounds and caused thick bushes to spring up as a protection. One of the knights, however, shot an arrow at random and wounded St. Giles. The king then made his way to the cave and was immediately impressed by the hermit's bearing but failed to persuade him to accept riches or even medical attention. Eventually he was induced to become first abbot of the noble Benedictine foundation at St-Gilles, near Nîmes. St. Giles is usually shown as an abbot, holding a crozier, with his hind either lying at his feet or leaping up to him.

GODWALL

Godwall has been identified with a Welsh bishop named Gudwal who became a wonder-working recluse and later migrated to Gulval, in Cornwall, where he established a monastery. More probably St. Godwall was a hermit, of strictly local reputation, who lived at Finstall, Worcestershire. The church at Finstall is dedicated to him, and he is incorrectly shown, in a wall-painting of about A.D. 1500 at the 'Commandery', Worcester, wearing the vestments of an archbishop.

GREGORY

Pope of Rome A.D. 590–604. He abandoned the prospect of a brilliant political career in order to become a monk, but his abilities were so obvious that two successive popes employed him as their representative at Constantinople. Gregory was forced against his will to become pope, but, once in office, he acted with the utmost vigour and determination, in spite of persistent ill health, at a time when the emperors had practically lost all control over Italy and society was crumbling. He negotiated with the Lombard invaders and organized systematic poor-relief as well as enforcing discipline on monks and clergy and striving to uphold the privileges of the Roman see. The spectacle of some Yorkshire boys exposed for sale in the market-place filled him with missionary zeal, and, though he was thwarted in his desire to undertake the conversion of England in person, he directed with minute care the expedition which he sent out under Augustine.

Gregory is reckoned as one of the Four Doctors of the Western Church, and the title receives justification not only from his commentaries on Scripture and pastoral treatises but also from the learned versatility shown by his vast correspondence. In addition, he founded choir-schools and was a reformer of the liturgy.

St. Gregory usually appears as a pope wearing the tiara and often holding a double or a triple cross. Sometimes a dove is shown near him, because the archdeacon Peter testified that he had seen the Holy Ghost in the form of a dove hovering over Gregory's head to inspire him as he wrote. Occasionally, as at Paignton, in Devon, or Wyverstone, in Suffolk, the 'Gregory Mass' is illustrated. Gregory is then seen kneeling before the altar and adoring the vision of the crucified Christ into whom the consecrated elements had been transformed in order to confirm the faith of a sceptical woman in the congregation.

GUDULE

Gudule (about A.D. 650–712) was educated by her godmother St. Gertrude at Nivelles Abbey, and then determined to pass her days in monastic seclusion near her home in Brabant. She gained a widespread reputation for piety and, after her relics had been transferred to Brussels, she became patron saint of that city. Representations of St. Gudule are very rare in England, but she is sometimes to be seen holding a lantern. This emblem refers to an occasion when a devil blew out her light, which was immediately rekindled by an angel. She is, as it were, one of the wise virgins[1] whose well-trimmed lamp may be extinguished by the powers of evil, unless the angels of God watch over her.

[1] St. Matthew xxv. 1.

GUTHLAC

A member of the royal family of Mercia, he at first gained distinction through his military exploits, but, deciding to devote himself to religion, he entered the monastery of Repton. Here readings were given from the lives of the hermits, and Guthlac felt drawn to imitate their austerities. He therefore retired to Crowland, in the Lincolnshire Fens, where, with two companions, he passed his days in ascetic simplicity and contemplation. He enjoyed heavenly visions but also had to combat demonic temptations and, when represented in Christian art, appears as a monk holding the scourge with which he flogged the Devil. As St. Guthlac's reputation grew other settlers arrived at Crowland, and a prosperous monastery was established there soon after his death (A.D. 714).

HARDULF (Eardulf). See ALKMUND.

HELEN

Mother of the emperor Constantine the Great. Her husband Constantius was required to divorce her for reasons of state policy, but her son treated her with the greatest respect and affection and converted her to Christianity. In A.D. 327, at the age of nearly eighty, she made an energetic and devout pilgrimage to Jerusalem, and founded several churches in Palestine, including one at Bethlehem and one on the Mount of Olives. But Helen's popularity in the Middle Ages rested on the tradition, which began to crystallize about seventy years after her death, that she was privileged to discover the cross of Christ on the site of the Passion. Certain unreliable English chroniclers, such as Geoffrey of Monmouth, gave currency to the idea that St. Helen was a daughter of Old King Cole, and a series of panels of stained glass at Ashton-under-Lyne that illustrate her life begins with the words 'Hic nascitur Elena Coyle regis filia'. She usually appears wearing a crown and holding a long cross, but is sometimes shown with short T-cross and book.

HENRY VI

Henry VI, king of England 1422–61, though never formally canonized, was venerated as a saint particularly in the north and east of England. His unfeigned and charitable piety, his fame as the recipient of divine visions, and the patience with which he endured the loss of his kingdom and the rigours of imprisonment, caused men soon to forget his deficiencies as a ruler. Moreover he was respected as a zealous patron of learning who watched over his foundations of Eton College and King's College, Cambridge, with constant and meticulous care. His tomb at Windsor became a place of pilgrimage, while in 1479 the archbishop of York was compelled by the government of Edward IV to restrain the faithful from venerating a statue of King Henry that had been set up in the Minster. A few years later Henry VII made a half-hearted attempt to secure his canonization, but, on discovering what fees were demanded, 'he thought it more necessary to keep his money at home, for the profit of his realm and country, rather than to impoverish his kingdom, for the gaining of a new holy day'.[1] King Henry VI is depicted on several Norfolk rood-screens, e.g. those at Barton Turf and Gateley, as a king of youthful appearance, holding orb and sceptre.

[1] Hall, *Chronicle*, p. 304.

HILARY

Bishop of Poitiers, A.D. 353–68. He was a convert who became a strict and pious layman and was appointed bishop by popular acclamation. His tenure of his see was troubled by controversies with the Arian heretics and, in particular, with Bishop Saturninus of Arles. Hilary was forced to go into exile in Asia for several years, and his absences from Poitiers were prolonged by his desire to preach what he held to be the true version of the Faith to the heretically inclined in Italy and Illyria. His doctrine gained general acceptance in Gaul and his writings, particularly his great work *On the Trinity*, introduced to the West the theological speculations of such Eastern Fathers as Athanasius. A tradition grew up that St. Hilary, when sailing back from exile, freed the island of Gallinaria from a plague of serpents by making the sign of the cross over them, and he is therefore invoked as patron against snakes.

HILDA

(A.D. 614–80.) A member of the royal house of Northumbria, she adopted a monastic life under the direction of St. Aidan. In 647 she was appointed abbess of a convent at Hartlepool, but, ten years later, she founded the great 'double' monastery, for both monks and nuns, at Whitby. The gentleness and grace of her rule earned for her the title of 'Mother', while, according to Bede, 'her prudence was such that not only humbler men in their need but sometimes even kings and princes sought and obtained her counsel'.[1] St. Hilda was a supporter of the Celtic rather than the Roman party in the English Church, and was therefore inclined to except St. Wilfrid from the scope of her universal charity.

[1] *Ecclesiastical History*, iv. 23.

HIPPOLYTUS

The Hippolytus of history was a bishop, possibly of
a Christian congregation at Portus, the harbour of
Rome, possibly claiming the see of Rome itself, and
at any rate a vigorous rival of Pope Callistus. He was
a scholar and Biblical critic of wide learning and interests but possessing little originality or critical
judgement; and he appears to have died as a martyr
in the mines of Sardinia to which he had been condemned (about A.D. 236). The Hippolytus of medieval
legend is, however, a mythical figure. He was described as the gaoler of St. Laurence and as converted
to Christianity by him. Hippolytus buried St. Laurence, whereupon the infuriated emperor Valerian
caused the family of Hippolytus to be beheaded and
the saint himself to be bound by the feet to the necks
of wild horses and torn asunder. This spectacular
execution was probably suggested to the composer of
the legend by the fact that the Greek name Hippolytus could mean 'torn by horses', and might also
recall the myth of Hippolytus, son of Theseus, who
was said to have met just such a death.

HONORIUS

A Roman who was consecrated fifth archbishop of Canterbury about A.D. 628. He was eager to extend the range of Christianity in England, and showed friendliness even to Aidan and others who followed Celtic rather than Roman usages. Honorius gave his support to the missionary endeavours of Felix in East Anglia, and settled Paulinus at Rochester when the death of King Edwin and the victories of the heathen Penda of Mercia caused Paulinus and Queen Ethelburga to leave Northumbria, but few details of his life are recorded. Honorius died in A.D. 653. He is occasionally portrayed in medieval glass, as in the choir at York Minster, with no characteristic emblem, but on the rood-screen at Wolborough, Devon, he holds a baker's shovel because he was selected by the bakers as their patron saint. It may be, however, that the Wolborough figure should be interpreted as St. Aubert, a bishop of Cambrai (A.D. 633–69) who was notable for the care with which he guided and encouraged those who had a vocation to the monastic life.

HUBERT

As bishop of Maestricht (A.D. 708) and afterwards of Liège, whither the see was transferred in 721, he was a vigorous missionary throughout Brabant and the Ardennes. This historical outline was filled in with picturesque legend that bears a close resemblance, in some points, to that of St. Eustace. St. Hubert becomes a son of the Duke of Aquitaine, mighty in arms, and devoted to the chase. One holy day, as people were going to church, Hubert set off to hunt, but was checked by the appearance of a stag bearing a shining crucifix between its horns. Hubert prostrated himself and from that moment changed his way of life. On the advice of St. Lambert, bishop of Maestricht, he went as a pilgrim to Rome where the pope, foreseeing Lambert's martyrdom, consecrated Hubert to succeed him. Amongst other miraculous events which occurred about the same time was the presentation by St. Peter of a key which not only indicated Hubert's episcopal authority but also gave him the power to cure lunatics. St. Hubert, who is patron saint of huntsmen, has a stag, or a stag with a crucifix between its antlers, as his emblem.

HUGH

A native of Burgundy, he joined the Canons Regular but transferred to the Carthusians. Henry II of England established a Charterhouse at Witham, Somerset, and Hugh was sent in answer to the king's request for an experienced man to be prior (A.D. 1175). He made such a good impression that he was promoted to be bishop of Lincoln eleven years later. Vigorous in upholding the privileges of the Church against the Crown, he was also a diligent pastor of his diocese and renowned for the humble devotion which caused him to minister to the diseased and bury the dead. He died in 1200 on his way back from France where he had been engaged in political negotiations and had also received an enthusiastic welcome at the mother house of the Carthusian Order. St. Hugh is represented as a bishop with a swan as his emblem, because a large swan was said to have followed him affectionately about when he was in residence at his palace at Stow.

HYBALD

Four Lincolnshire churches are dedicated to St. Hybald. He is a shadowy figure, but a chance reference in Bede's *Church History*[1] indicates that he was a pious hermit who became abbot of Bardney.

[1] iv. 3.

IGNATIUS

Ignatius, third bishop of Antioch, was called also
'Theophorus' ('God-bearer' or 'Carried by God') and
this led to the belief that he was the 'little child' whom
Jesus set in the midst of the disciples when they were
disputing about precedence—'and taking him in his
arms he said unto them, Whosoever shall receive one
of such little children in my name, receiveth me'.[1]
Ignatius was arrested about A.D. 108 and taken as a
prisoner to Rome. During his journey he set an
example of constancy in accepting, and indeed eagerly
welcoming, the prospect of martyrdom, and he found
opportunity to send seven letters, one to Rome and
the rest to the churches in various towns of Asia
Minor through which he had passed. These letters,
besides thanking the recipients for the kindness which
they had shown to him, emphasized the need for
episcopal government if the churches were to safe-
guard the truth committed to them and avoid the
seductive errors of heresy. St. Ignatius is one of
the Fathers of the Church who was disregarded in the
Middle Ages. He appears, however, in seventeenth-
century glass in the chapel at Magdalen College,
Oxford, and finds a place in the calendar of the 1928
Prayer Book.

[1] St. Mark ix. 36.

INA

Ina, king of Wessex A.D. 688–726, though never formally canonized, gained widespread repute for saintliness of life as well as for warlike vigour. He devoted much time to the foundation and strengthening of monasteries in the west of England and to problems of Church organization and discipline. Towards the end of his life he abandoned the cares of kingship and retired, with his Queen Ethelburga, to Rome, where he practised a pious asceticism and died in A.D. 730.

IRENAEUS

A native of Asia Minor, he removed to Gaul and was elected bishop of Lyons in A.D. 177. He strove to secure the peace of the Church in times of difficulty and ferment, as is shown by his effort to restrain Pope Victor from picking a quarrel with the bishops of Asia Minor over the method of fixing the date of Easter. He was also a patron of missionaries, but his fame rests on his achievements as a scholar whose greatest work was a learned and systematic defence of orthodox Christianity against many varieties of heretical opinion. Irenaeus died about A.D. 203, and an unreliable tradition, which, however, gained wide acceptance, declared him to be a martyr. For all his distinction he attracted little popular attention in England during the Middle Ages, but is portrayed in seventeenth-century glass at Magdalen College, Oxford, and appears in the calendar of the 1928 Prayer Book.

IVES

According to a legend, perhaps invented by the monks of Ramsey in the eleventh century, St. Ives or Ivo, was a Persian bishop who departed by way of Asia, Rome, and Gaul to preach the Gospel in Britain. He settled in the neighbourhood of Huntingdon and is commemorated by the name of the town of St. Ives, where he was buried. The Cornish St. Ives (Ia) is a different person. Her story makes her the daughter of an Irish nobleman and relates that she sailed over to Cornwall on a leaf, being one of a considerable party of saintly immigrants who, in miraculous fashion, made their way across the seas from Ireland to Cornwall about the same time. A more clearly historical character, but apparently little honoured in England, is St. Ives of Brittany, who gained local renown for his honesty as a lawyer:

> Lo ! a marvel past belief,
> A barrister who's not a thief ! [1]

Later, after his ordination, he was distinguished for the self-sacrificing humility with which he ministered to his parishioners and for his miraculous powers of healing the diseased. He died in A.D. 1303.

---

[1] Advocatus et non latro,
Res miranda populo.

JAMES THE DEACON

James the Deacon is shown, in glass that has been renewed, at York Minster, and perhaps elsewhere in the county. According to Bede's *Ecclesiastical History*[1] James showed great zeal in supporting the missionary endeavours of Paulinus. When Paulinus, in dismay at the confusion which followed the death of King Edwin, decided to return to Kent, James courageously stayed behind at York to teach and baptize. He lived to a great age and, being an Italian and a skilled musician, zealously instructed his people in the use of the Roman chant.

[1] ii. 16 and 20.

JAMES THE GREAT

The son of Zebedee and brother of St. John was one of the three privileged apostles chosen to be with Christ on such occasions as the Transfiguration and the Agony in the Garden of Gethsemane. As one of the leaders of the church, he was beheaded by order of Herod Agrippa I in A.D. 42. Later tradition described missionary labours in Spain and told how, after St. James's execution, disciples placed his body in a ship lacking sail or rudder and, committing themselves to the seas, arrived on the Spanish coast. He therefore became the patron saint of Spain, and his shrine at Compostella was distinguished by many miracles and became a famous place of pilgrimage. In order to visit it, Englishmen were prepared even to withstand the rigours of a voyage across the Bay of Biscay that are feelingly alluded to by a fifteenth-century writer:

> Men may leve alle gamys
> That saylen to Seynt Jamys.
> Ffor many a man it gramys[1]
> When they begin to sayle.

St. James was so closely linked with the idea of pilgrimages that he regularly appears dressed as a pilgrim with staff, wallet, and a scallop-shell in his hat. He is, in fact, a pilgrim to his own shrine.

[1] Vexes.

135

JAMES THE LESS

James, 'the Lord's brother',[1] was popularly identified with James the son of Alphaeus who finds a place in the Gospel lists of the twelve Apostles. Becoming head of the church at Jerusalem, he presided at the council (Acts xv) held to consider how far the Gentile Christians should be required to conform to Jewish customs, and he treated St. Paul with authority when advising him to counteract the misapprehensions and hatred of zealous Jews by undertaking the performance of a Nazirite vow. St. James earned the title of 'the Just',[2] and his knees were said to have become hardened like those of a camel by reason of his assiduity in prayer. According to the Jewish historian Josephus,[3] he was charged before the court of the Sanhedrin with 'breaking the laws', and was stoned. But Christian tradition followed the account of Hegesippus,[4] who records that St. James was flung by the Scribes and Pharisees from the pinnacle of the Temple and then, since he survived the fall, was killed by a blow on the head from a fuller's club. Therefore the usual emblem of St. James the Less is a fuller's club, though occasionally he holds a sword.

[1] Galatians i. 19.

[2] He is so described by Hegesippus, who is acclaimed as the Father of Church History and who wrote in the middle of the second century.

[3] *Antiquities*, xx. ix. 1.

[4] Quoted in Eusebius' *Ecclesiastical History*, ii. 23.

JANUARIUS

Several martyrs bore this name, and traditions about
them are frequently confused. The most famous is
the patron saint of Naples, where some of his blood
is kept and is miraculously subject to periodic lique-
faction. He is said to have been a bishop of Bene-
ventum who was beheaded during an outbreak of
persecution about A.D. 305. St. Januarius is very
rarely depicted in England: he appears as a bishop
without characteristic emblem.

JEROME

(A.D. 346–420.) Born at Stridon, in Dalmatia, he completed his education at Rome and was baptized there. He settled at Aquileia with a company of friends all eager for sacred learning and subject to ascetic discipline, but Jerome, who possessed the faculty of inspiring passionate dislike as well as passionate loyalty, found himself compelled to retire to Antioch. Ill health, and a vision in which he felt himself condemned before the throne of God as being a Ciceronian rather than a Christian, led him to renounce classical studies and retire to the Syrian desert where, as he wrote, 'my limbs were graceless and rough with sackcloth and my squalid skin became black as an Ethiopian's'.[1] He returned to Rome in 381 and was active in the production of Biblical translations and commentaries and in promoting monasticism, but disputes arose and he settled at Bethlehem. Here, in spite of the demands of a voluminous correspondence and the cares arising from the supervision of his monks, he devoted his energies without respite to works of Christian scholarship and, in particular, to his great task of translating the Old Testament from Hebrew into Latin (the 'Vulgate'). Jerome is de-

[1] *Letter* xxii. 7.

servedly reckoned as one of the four Doctors of the Western Church. He usually wears a cardinal's hat and holds a book or inkhorn. Frequently a lion appears near him, in allusion to the story that a lion with a thorn in its foot found its way to Jerome's monastery and, thankful for medical attention, remained there as a tame and faithful servant.

JEROŇ (HIERON)

A Scottish priest who worked with success as a missionary in Holland until he was seized by Danish raiders and beheaded, about A.D. 856. He is invoked for aid in finding lost property. Jeron occurs several times on East Anglian rood-screens. He wears a robe or priest's cassock over armour, while a falcon perches on his left arm. This is a punning allusion to his name, since Hieron suggests 'hierax', the Greek word for a falcon.

JOACHIM

The second-century *Protevangelium of James*[1] records that the father of the Virgin Mary was named Joachim. He and his wife Anna bewailed their childlessness, and Anna vowed: 'If I bring forth either male or female, I will bring it for a gift unto the Lord my God, and it shall be ministering unto Him all the days of its life.' Therefore, when Mary was three years old, Joachim and Anna took her, with an escort of maidens bearing lamps, up to the Temple and presented her there, whereat 'the Lord put grace upon her and she danced with her feet and all the house of Israel loved her. And her parents gat them down marvelling and praising the Lord God.' St. Joachim is occasionally depicted with the Virgin and St. Anne. In the Cathedral at Bury St. Edmund's he holds a lamb, the symbol of purity and innocence.

[1] Translated by M. R. James in *The Apocryphal New Testament* (Oxford, 1924), pp. 38–49.

JOHN THE APOSTLE

 John the son of Zebedee, a fisherman and a Galilean, was one of the small inner group of Christ's disciples privileged to accompany the Master during some, at least, of His retirements for solemn prayer and communion with the Father. John is not mentioned in the Fourth Gospel,[1] but is usually identified with the author of that Gospel as well as with 'the disciple whom Jesus loved'.[2] In spite of powerful criticisms first advanced in the third century by Bishop Dionysius of Alexandria, the book of Revelation has also been commonly assigned to him.

In the Acts of the Apostles St. John appears, together with St. Peter, healing the lame man at the Beautiful Gate of the Temple (iii. 1–10) and bestowing the gift of the Holy Ghost on Philip's Samaritan converts. Thereafter he becomes the subject of dubious and fragmentary traditions. He is said to have been miraculously preserved from death when thrown into a cauldron of boiling oil at Rome during the persecution of Domitian, then to have been banished to the island of Patmos and afterwards to have spent the closing years of his long life at Ephesus.

[1] Except for the reference to the 'sons of Zebedee' in John xxi. 2.

[2] St. John xiii. 23, &c.

St. John is depicted by the medieval artists as a young man, distinguished from the other apostles by his lack of a beard. His usual emblem is a cup, with a snake or dragon emerging from it, because of the story that a priest of Diana challenged him to drink a cup of poison which John rendered harmless by blessing it with the sign of the cross. But he often appears with, or is represented by, an eagle. To each of the Evangelists was early assigned one of the four symbolic creatures drawn by the author of Revelation[1] from the imagery of Ezekiel:[2] 'and the first creature was like a lion, and the second creature like a calf, and the third creature had a face as of a man, and the fourth creature was like a flying eagle'. The eagle was thought to be appropriate to St. John because, as Jerome explained,[3] he 'soared aloft' to contemplate the divine nature of the Saviour.

[1] iv. 7.   [2] i. 5.
[3] *Commentary on Ezekiel*, i.

JOHN THE BAPTIST

His story as told in the Gospels was sufficiently dramatic to need no embellishment. The account of his proclamation of the coming of Christ and his reluctance to baptize Him is given by St. Mark at the beginning of his Gospel (i. 1–11), and St. Matthew[1] and St. Luke[2] offer a parallel but rather fuller narrative, whereas St. John[3] puts the 'witness of John' after the baptism of Christ. The writer of the Fourth Gospel omits the colourful story, recorded by the other three evangelists, of St. John the Baptist's death and the implacable enmity of Herodias. The Baptist is usually represented as 'clothed with camel's hair, and a leather girdle about his loins', and as holding a lamb,[4] in allusion to his exclamation at the sight of Jesus, 'Behold, the Lamb of God.'

[1] iii. 1–15.　　　　[2] iii. 1–17.　　　　[3] i. 19–35.
[4] Often shown with the banner which symbolizes the Resurrection.

JOHN OF BEVERLEY

Educated at Whitby Abbey, he gave himself up to contemplation, study, and teaching, and had Bede as one of his pupils. He was appointed bishop of Hexham in A.D. 687, and transferred, eighteen years later, to York, gaining a reputation in both sees for amiable manners, unaffected piety, and pastoral zeal. He founded a double monastery at Beverley, which became an important ecclesiastical centre during his lifetime and a much-frequented shrine, famous for its miracles, after his death (A.D. 721). St. John of Beverley is shown at Hexham and elsewhere as an archbishop, but without distinctive emblem.

JOHN OF BRIDLINGTON

John of Bridlington (d. 1379) was a Canon Regular, and eventually prior of St. Mary, Bridlington. He gained some repute for prophetic verses concerning the course of English history that were, perhaps falsely, assigned to him, and was more widely renowned for his life of piety signalized by miracles which, continuing after his death, made his shrine a favourite place of pilgrimage. He is occasionally depicted by the medieval artist, as at Hempstead, Norfolk, and Morley, Derbyshire, in the habit of a canon and holding a crozier or a long cross and a fish.

JOHN CHRYSOSTOM

John Chrysostom was a lawyer of Antioch who, partly through the influence of St. Basil, abandoned the prospect of a brilliant career, received baptism, and retired to lead a life of extreme asceticism in the Syrian mountains. But his health broke down and he went back to Antioch where he was ordained and immediately won a great reputation, as well as the nickname Chrysostom ('Gold-Mouth'), for his eloquence as a preacher. He was active also with the pen, and is said to have written systematic commentaries on the whole of Scripture, besides reforming the liturgy of the Eastern Church. In A.D. 398 John Chrysostom was consecrated, much against his will, as bishop of Constantinople. He was welcomed with enthusiasm, but soon incurred some hostility for his condemnation of the magnificent establishment which his predecessor had maintained and for the firm discipline which he imposed on the clergy. But in other quarters he was revered for the practical sympathy which he showed to the poor and for his zeal in organizing missions to the Goths and Scythians who lived on the banks of the Danube. He was in high favour at court until he offended the empress Eudoxia, who thereupon worked with vigour and skill to secure his banishment. A council held in A.D. 403 under the presidency of Theophilus, bishop of Alexandria, who also was jealous of Chrysostom, deposed him, but the popular clamour was such that the empress became alarmed and he was recalled. However, violent partisanship continued and he was again exiled, being finally sent to a remote and bleak part of the Caucasus where he succumbed to his hardships in A.D. 407. St. John Chrysostom was largely disregarded by medieval churchmen in England, but several dedications to him were made in the nineteenth century and his name appears in the calendar of the 1928 Prayer Book.

JOHN SCHORNE

John Schorne (d. 1308) was rector of North Marston, Buckinghamshire, and though never formally canonized, was honoured for his miracles and piety. It was said that, because of his assiduity in prayer, his knees had become hardened and horny, and a spring was pointed out which he had caused to burst forth in a time of drought and whose waters were a sovereign specific against gout. But his greatest feat was that he conjured the Devil into a boot, and he is represented, as on the screens at Cawston and Gateley in Norfolk, wearing academic cap and robes and holding a boot from which the Devil's head projects.

JOSEPH

HUSBAND OF THE VIRGIN MARY

To the somewhat meagre notices about St. Joseph
that are contained in the Gospels of St. Matthew and
St. Luke a wealth of vivid detail was added by such
apocryphal works as the second-century *Protevangelium
of James* and the fifth-century *History of the Death
of Joseph*.[1] According to traditions found therein,
the High Priest was commanded by an angel to call
together all suitable widowers in order that a husband might be chosen for the Virgin Mary. Each of
the widowers was required to bring a rod with him
into the Temple since the Lord was about to 'show a
sign', and from Joseph's rod there flew a dove which
settled on his head, thus assuring him of God's
favour. Joseph was at first reluctant to take Mary as
his wife, saying, 'I have sons and am an old man,
while she is a girl. I shall become a laughing-stock
to the children of Israel', but the High Priest overcame such objections by pointing out the necessity
for obeying the Divine Will. At the birth of Christ,
Joseph had a vision of the whole of creation 'standing still in amazement' until 'of a sudden things
moved onwards in their course'.

After the flight into Egypt and the return to
Nazareth, Joseph continued to work vigorously at
his trade, but, on reaching the age of a hundred and
eleven, he received warning that his death was at
hand. He then fell into a state of terror and distress,
but Jesus comforted him, saved his body from cor-

[1] See *The Apocryphal New Testament*, translated by M. R.
James.

ruption, and entrusted his soul to the care of the angelic host led by Michael and Gabriel. These apocryphal stories were without influence on English ecclesiastical art, and St. Joseph is seldom shown except as a figure in such Biblical scenes as the Nativity or the Flight into Egypt. His popularity as a patron who ensures a happy death for his devotees did not develop until late in the medieval period.

JOSEPH OF ARIMATHAEA

Joseph of Arimathaea was the wealthy disciple who obtained the body of Jesus from Pilate and laid it in his own newly made sepulchre.[1] Later legend told how, together with St. Philip and others, he collected some of the blood of Jesus in a precious vessel and brought this Holy Grail to Glastonbury, thus becoming the first Christian missionary to reach Britain. When he arrived at Glastonbury, the staff which he was holding suddenly budded and burst into blossom as a sign that his journey's end was reached. Joseph of Arimathaea may therefore have a pot of ointment and a budding staff as his emblems. Occasionally, however, he holds the two cruets which, according to one version of his story, contained the blood and sweat of Christ and were buried with Joseph in his grave.

[1] St. Matthew xxvii. 57–60.

JOSES. See MARY, THE MOTHER OF JAMES.

JUDE

Jude (Thaddaeus), the brother of St. James the Less and son of Mary, wife of Cleopas, is one of the Apostles who play no individual part in the Gospel story. According to the *Golden Legend*, Jude took a letter from Jesus to Abgar, king of Edessa, and afterwards preached in Mesopotamia. Together with Simon he went on to Persia, where the idols were overthrown and idol-worship confounded so decisively that the pagan priests rushed at the Apostles and 'hewed them to death'. St. Jude usually holds a boat, but sometimes he bears an emblem, such as club or carpenter's square, which is more commonly assigned to one of the other Apostles.

JULIAN

Several saints bore this name, and their stories were often confused. A Julian was said to have been sent out from Rome to Gaul and to have succeeded in converting the whole tribe of Cenomanni, becoming the first bishop of Le Mans. Another Julian was honoured in the Middle Ages as a devoted physician who, together with his wife Basilissa, established a hospital at Alexandria and suffered as a martyr under Diocletian. But he has, perhaps, little claim to be regarded as an historical personage.

More famous was Julian Hospitaller, a mythical character whose remarkable legend appealed to Flaubert and was retold by him. The story ran that he was a young man addicted to the chase, who was informed by a hunted deer that he would slay his father and mother. Julian, alarmed at this portent, ran away from home and entered the service of a prince to whom he commended himself by reason of his vigour and bravery. He received, by way of reward, marriage with a rich widow who owned a castle. In the course of time Julian's mother and father arrived at the castle, searching for their son. They were hospitably received by his wife and put to rest in her room, while she went to church. Julian came in and, imagining that he had caught his wife in adultery, killed the two figures that were lying on the bed. When he discovered the truth, he was horrified and resolved to lead a life of penance and good works. His wife insisted on accompanying him, and they founded a hospice on the bank of a wide river which they helped people to cross. After some years of this labour, Julian was one day hailed by an unattractive stranger, frozen and diseased. Julian, moved by pity, laid him in his own bed, whereat the stranger was transfigured in shining light and declared that he was a messenger sent by Christ to announce to Julian that his penance was accepted. Shortly afterwards Julian and his wife died. St. Julian Hospitaller is seldom represented in English churches. His emblem is an oar, because of his activities as a ferryman.

JULIANA

Two saints of the same name, Juliana of Cumae and Juliana of Nicomedia, are confused and neither is a very substantial person in history. Of Juliana of Nicomedia the *Golden Legend* records that she was betrothed to the governor of the district but refused to marry him until he had embraced the Christian faith. She was cast into prison, where she was tempted by the Devil, in the likeness of an angel, to sacrifice to idols with a view to escaping torture, but through prayer she was strengthened to question and overcome him. She was then beheaded after exemplary torments. St. Juliana is represented as flogging the Devil or holding him in chains.

JULITTA. See CYRIAC.

KENELM

Traditionally the son of Kenulf, king of Mercia, whom he succeeded on the throne in A.D. 822, Kenelm was only a child and was placed in the care of his sister Quenthritha, who coveted the throne for herself. An attempt to kill Kenelm by poison failed, but a court official was prevailed upon to take him away to a wood at Clent and cut off his head. Kenelm, who had been forewarned of his fate in a dream, died calmly whilst reciting the *Te Deum*. His body was conveyed in state to Winchcombe Abbey, and during the funeral service Quenthritha's eyes fell out as punishment for her crime. St. Kenelm has no characteristic emblem. On the west front of Wells Cathedral he[1] appears as a young king trampling on the prostrate figure of Quenthritha.

[1] The identification is probable but by no means certain.

KENTIGERN

Kentigern (Mungo) was a missionary bishop of singular charm and piety who worked in the Strathclyde district of Scotland. He founded a monastery at Glasgow and earned respect and popularity, but civil strife and the opposition of paganism caused him to migrate to Cumberland and thence to St. Asaph in North Wales. Recalled in A.D. 574 by Rhydderch who had succeeded to the throne and defeated the heathen in battle, he went back to the Strathclyde district, settling at Hoddam, Dumfriesshire, where Rhydderch and his people joyfully submitted themselves to Kentigern's guidance. He later returned to Glasgow and was visited there by St. Columba. St. Kentigern is represented as a bishop, and may hold a salmon with a ring in its mouth. This emblem refers to one of the most famous of his miracles. King Rhydderch happened to notice on the finger of a sleeping knight a golden ring which he had given to his wife. Suspecting her of adultery, he stealthily drew off the ring and threw it into the sea. When challenged to produce the ring, the Queen appealed to Kentigern for help, whereat the bishop ordered her to set anglers to work and bring him the first fish that was caught. A salmon soon came to hand and, when opened, proved to contain the lost ring, which was then shown to the gratified king. Kentigern died, at a great age, about A.D. 612.

KYNEBURGA

Kyneburga, a daughter of Penda, king of Mercia, married Aldfrid, prince of Northumbria, but, with her husband's consent, she soon returned to Mercia and became abbess of a nunnery at Castor, near Peterborough. No details of her life are recorded, except that she was present in A.D. 657 at the consecration of St. Peter's Minster, now Peterborough Cathedral. Castor church is dedicated to her. There was formerly a Kyneburga's church at Gloucester also, but the saint thereby commemorated appears to have been a different person, the sister of Osric (who was prime minister to King Ethelred of Mercia) and first abbess of Gloucester Abbey which Osric founded in A.D. 681.

LAMBERT

Lambert became bishop of Maestricht, of which city he was a native, in A.D. 670. Five years later, on the death of King Childeric II, he was expelled and submitted himself to rigorous monastic discipline, but Pepin of Heristal restored him to his see where 'he shone by word and by ensample in all virtue'.[1] He was stabbed as an act of revenge for the death of two brothers who had repeatedly plundered the church and were slain in an affray by the bishop's partisans. Representations of St. Lambert are very rare in England. Where he appears, as in a window made up of German glass in St. Mary's, Shrewsbury, it is as a bishop holding a sword.

[1] *Golden Legend*, v. 149.

LAUD

Laud (Lo), a sixth-century bishop of Coutances, is commemorated by the town in Normandy which bears his name and is honoured by a church dedication at Sherington, Buckinghamshire, but nothing is known of his life beyond the fact that he was a regular attendant at successive church councils held at Orléans for the purpose of regulating ecclesiastical discipline.

LAURENCE

Laurence, the most popular of all the Roman martyrs, was one of the seven deacons of Rome under Pope Sixtus II. In A.D. 258 the emperor Valerian ordained punishment for officials of the Church and Sixtus was put to death. Laurence was detained in custody by the prefect of Rome who demanded that he should bring forth the treasures of the Church; but when Laurence produced not the expected silver and gold but certain poor persons for whom the Church was caring, the exasperated prefect, according to tradition, sentenced him to be roasted over a slow fire. St. Laurence is therefore represented in the vestments of a deacon and holding a gridiron. At Ludlow a window dating from about 1450 gives twenty-seven scenes from his life and miracles.

LEGER

Leger (Leodegarius) was appointed bishop of Autun
in A.D. 660 when the city, and indeed the whole of
France, was vexed by political and personal rivalries.
Leger became head of the party of nobles who desired to limit the king's prerogatives, and, as such,
was bitterly opposed by the royal chamberlain Ebroin.
King Childeric II suspected the bishop of plotting to
dethrone him, so Leger was ordered to retire into
monastic seclusion at Luxeuil, but, on the succession
to the throne of Theoderic III, was able to return to
Autun. Ebroin, however, sent an expedition against
the city, and Leger, who gave himself up so that the
other inhabitants might be spared, had his eyes put
out and was held in custody, suffering barbarous
tortures before he was beheaded. His body was
transferred to Poitiers, and miracles proclaimed its
sanctity, but St. Leger's martydom was a matter of
politics rather than religion. His emblem is the
auger, with which his eyes were bored out.[1]

[1] See Frontispiece.

LEO

After proving his capabilities as archdeacon of Rome, Leo was elected pope in A.D. 440. The Western Empire was in a state of collapse by reason of the inefficiency of its rulers and the savage onslaughts of barbarian hordes, while the Church was enfeebled owing to bitter disputes on points of doctrine. Leo's vigour and constancy made him the one figure in Europe around whom the forces of civilization could rally, and he gained great prestige in 451 by courageously going forth, accompanied only by two other unarmed ambassadors, to meet Attila, king of the Huns, whom he persuaded to withdraw from Italy. Four years later he succeeded also in restraining the Vandals under Gaiseric from the wanton destruction of Rome. Leo's interests may be judged from his letters and sermons which are mainly concerned with the practical details of Christian duty and with the claim that he was heir to the peculiar privileges of St. Peter and was entitled, by virtue of the command 'Feed my sheep',[1] to assert a far-flung control over the Christians of the Empire. When he treats of theological matters it is to affirm in clear and unspeculative terms the orthodox doctrine of the Incarnation as against any current opinions which appeared to disregard either the humanity or the divinity of Christ. Leo's memory was highly honoured at Rome, and he received the title of 'The Great', but he failed to secure popularity as a patron saint in England. He is shown, however, in a window of the Lady Chapel at Wells Cathedral.

[1] St. John xxi. 18.

LEONARD

Leonard (about A.D. 485–560) was brought up at the court of Clovis I of France and, according to his legend, obtained the king's permission to release every prisoner whom he visited. He felt himself called to a monastic life and, after preaching the Gospel in Guyenne, became the first abbot of Noblac monastery, near Limoges. St. Leonard earned great popularity as patron of prisoners, since it was said that anyone in prison who called on his name was freed from all bonds and fetters. He is depicted as an abbot, holding a chain or fetter.

LONGINUS

Apocryphal legend bestows this name on the soldier who pierced the side of Christ with his spear,[1] and the same name is assigned to the centurion who, when present at the Crucifixion, was converted, exclaiming: 'Truly this man was the Son of God.'[2] Longinus was said to have been beheaded for fearlessly acknowledging his faith. He was seldom represented by medieval artists but occasionally appears as a soldier holding a spear.

[1] St. John xix. 34.   [2] St. Mark xv. 39.

LOUIS

Louis IX, king of France A.D. 1226–70. Benefiting by the influence of his mother, Blanche of Castile, he devoted himself to carrying out his official duties with humility and justice and to an enthusiastic but disciplined piety. He was a patron of the Friars and a founder of churches, of which the most famous is the Sainte-Chapelle at Paris, built to house the Crown of Thorns, part of the Cross, the spearhead which pierced the side of Christ, and other relics. While maintaining his royal position with much splendour, he habitually practised such acts of personal charity as ministering with his own hands to poor persons who lay sick in hospital. Louis was taken prisoner when on a Crusade in 1250 but was ransomed; in 1270 he set out again at the head of a new Crusade but died at Tunis. He is shown as a king holding a crown of thorns and a cross or three nails. Occasionally the lilies of France are added.

LUCIAN

Several canonized saints bear this name, including Lucian of Antioch, the Arian scholar and philosopher, who atoned for his heretical teaching by patiently enduring a long imprisonment and meeting a martyr's death in A.D. 312. But the Lucian who is commemorated in the Anglican calendar on 8 January and has a church dedication at Farnley Tyas, Yorkshire, is a somewhat shadowy figure. He is said to have come to France with St. Denis and, after preaching the gospel at Beauvais and becoming bishop there, to have suffered as a martyr, perhaps about A.D. 290.

LUCY

A famous martyr of Syracuse who suffered in the persecution ordered by the emperor Diocletian about A.D. 303. Her romantic *Acts* tell a colourful story, according to which Lucy dedicated herself to a life of virginity, broke off her engagement to marry, and disposed of her considerable property in alms-giving. Her rejected suitor complained to the governor, Paschasius, whose efforts at forcibly persuading her to sacrifice to idols were miraculously thwarted. Lucy survived and continued to prophesy even when a sword was thrust through her neck, but, after the recall of Paschasius to Rome, she offered up her thanksgiving to God and died. St. Lucy is shown clasping a sword or with a sword driven through her neck. Or she may hold a book with her eyes lying on it; for the name Lucy suggested light (*lux*) and, as she was therefore invoked by sufferers from eye-trouble, stories grew up to the effect that her eyes were gouged out but miraculously restored to her in enhanced beauty.

LUKE

The writer of the Third Gospel and the Acts of the Apostles accompanied St. Paul as a 'fellow-worker'[1] during the latter stages of the Apostle's missionary journeys and ministered to him when he was in prison at Rome. The details of Luke's subsequent career are quite uncertain. He may have engaged in missionary labours in Greece and met a martyr's death there. From St. Paul's reference[2] to the 'beloved physician' it has been assumed that Luke was a doctor and attempts have been made, with variable success, to discover medical terms in his writings. The alternative tradition that he was a painter, who converted many by showing them his attractive portraits of Christ and the Virgin Mary, may date from as early as the sixth century A.D. St. Luke is usually depicted with, or represented by, his symbol as an evangelist.[3] This is an ox, often winged, and was explained as being the sacrificial beast, appropriate to a Gospel which stressed the priesthood of Christ.

[1] Philemon 24.   [2] Colossians iv. 14.
[3] See note on St. John.

MAGNUS

Several saints bore this name, but the one to whom three English churches[1] are dedicated is Magnus, earl of Orkney. As a result of the jealous intrigues of his cousin Haakon, who shared with him the sovereignty over the Orkneys, he was forced by Magnus Barefoot, king of Norway, to join in a piratical expedition that sailed down the west coast of Scotland as far south as the Menai Straits. Magnus of Orkney declined, however, to attack those with whom he had no quarrel, but he refuted a charge of cowardice by remaining at the ship's prow calmly chanting the psalter during the heat of the battle. He escaped to the Scottish court, but later returned to the Orkneys where his popularity so infuriated Haakon that he caused Magnus to be treacherously overpowered and put to death during a conference held on the island of Egilshay to decide terms of peace between the rivals (about A.D. 1107).

[1] There is some doubt concerning the church of St. Magnus the Martyr in the City of London, since it appears to be mentioned fifty years or so before the death of Magnus, earl of Orkney.

MALO

Malo (Machutus) was one of the many Welshmen who settled and worked in Brittany during the sixth century A.D. While still a boy, he became a pupil of the monastery of Aleth, now called St. Malo, and was providentially saved from drowning by the support of a floating heap of seaweed one day when he had been cut off by a sudden rise of the tide. After living for some years as a hermit on a nearby island, he became bishop of Aleth, receiving his consecration to the episcopate in Wales. Persecution by a hostile king as well as ecclesiastical jealousies caused him to retire from his see, but he was able to return before his death and add further to his reputation for unassuming sanctity.

MARGARET (OF ANTIOCH IN PISIDIA)

This very popular and celebrated patroness, guardian of women in childbirth, is a shadowy figure and her story, as recounted in the *Golden Legend*, lacks historical substance. Her beauty is said to have attracted the attention of the prefect Olybrius, who desired her in marriage. But when he was questioning her about her name and condition, he discovered that she was a Christian and therefore caused her to be seized and tortured. While she was in  prison, she was assailed by a fiendish dragon—one version had it that she was swallowed by a dragon—but the beast was overcome and disappeared as soon as she made the sign of the cross. Margaret remained unmoved by further torments and five thousand people were converted at the sight of her constancy, but finally she was beheaded. St. Margaret's regular emblem is her dragon, and she is often shown thrusting the staff of a long cross into its mouth. A few of the 260 church dedications to St. Margaret may be intended to honour St. Margaret of Scotland (A.D. 1045–93) who, by her piety and prudent statecraft, strengthened the realm of her husband, King Malcolm III.

MARK

Mark the Evangelist is usually identified with **Mark**, the cousin of St. Barnabas, who accompanied Barnabas and Paul on their missionary journey to Cyprus but, to Paul's great indignation, left them at Perga in Pamphylia and went back to Jerusalem. He later revisited Cyprus in company with Barnabas and, after some years, regained the friendship of St. Paul, attending him in his Roman imprisonment and being praised as a 'comfort' to him[1] and a 'fellow-worker'.[2] In the First Epistle of St. Peter[3] there is a reference to 'Mark, my son', and early tradition connected him

closely with this Apostle, making him the 'interpreter of Peter'[4] and describing his Gospel as based on Peter's reminiscences. He probably accompanied St. Peter to Rome and he is said also to have been the first bishop of Alexandria. St. Mark, like the other Evangelists, derives his emblem from the description of the 'four living creatures' who utter

[1] Colossians iv. 11.　　　[2] Philemon 24.　　　[3] v. 13.
[4] So Papias, a second-century bishop of Hierapolis in Phrygia, as quoted by Eusebius in his *Ecclesiastical History*, iii. 39.

167

ceaseless praises before the throne of God.[5] To Mark was assigned the lion,[6] which churchmen explained as typifying the Resurrection, since the lion's whelps were believed to remain dead for three days after their birth and to be revived by the roaring of their parents.

[5] Revelation iv. 7. [6] Often a winged lion.

MARTHA

The sister of Lazarus and Mary of Bethany, she was 'careful and troubled about many things' when providing hospitable entertainment for Jesus.[1] She was present at the raising of Lazarus, but nothing is known of her later history except a tradition that she, together with her brother and sister and other companions, was placed by the Jews in an unseaworthy boat and forced to sail away from Joppa. However, the party reached the coast of Cyprus in safety or, according to a later version of the same story, arrived at the mouth of the Rhone and engaged in missionary labours around Marseilles. St. Martha is rarely represented in English churches and, when she does appear, it is usually in glass imported from the Continent. She may hold a ladle or housewife's keys; elsewhere she sprinkles holy water on a dragon and thus confounds it.

[1] St. Luke x. 38–42; St. John xii. 2.

MARTIN

This much-loved saint was born in Pannonia (Hungary) about A.D. 316 and trained to follow his father's profession as a soldier. Whilst still a boy he showed those qualities of self-denial and humility which marked his career. The story is told that, one bitter winter's day when Martin was with his regiment at Amiens, he took pity on a beggar whom all were passing by and, having no money in his purse, divided his cloak with his sword and gave half to the beggar. The next night he dreamed that he saw Christ wearing this half-cloak, and shortly afterwards he was baptized. A year or two later he left the army and, after remaining for a time under the guidance of Hilary, bishop of Poitiers, founded the monastery of Ligugé. Martin's reputation for piety became such that he was, against his desires, consecrated bishop of Tours (A.D. 371). He continued to live under a severe monastic rule nearby, at Marmoutier, but was vigorous in preaching the Gospel throughout his diocese, calmly facing many difficulties caused both by pagans and by heretics. He became famous for supernatural powers whereby he was enabled to raise the dead to life, remain unharmed by fire, exercise authority over animals, and repel the onslaughts made by devils in manifold disguises. But the abiding impression which he left was of one who, as St. Ambrose said of him, 'raised the banners of pity'[1] in a harsh

[1] *Golden Legend*, vi. 157.

age. St. Martin is sometimes depicted as a bishop offering alms to the needy; or his gift of half his cloak to the beggar may be illustrated. Occasionally he has a goose as his emblem because his feast day (11 November) comes at a time when geese are killed and eaten.

MARY THE VIRGIN

The mother of Christ, to whom her Son would refuse no petition, was naturally pre-eminent among the patron saints whom the medieval church delighted to honour. As early as the second century A.D. she was regarded as Eve's antitype, bringing salvation to the human race instead of the curse brought by Eve; and, about the same time, picturesque accounts[1] of her dedication in the Temple by her parents Joachim and Anna and of her betrothal to Joseph began to circulate. But it was after the condemnation of the Nestorians at the Council of Ephesus (A.D. 431), and the consequent emphasis on the divinity as opposed to the humanity of Christ, that devotion to the Virgin quickened and she was acclaimed as the Mother of God, 'the only bridge between God and man'. Thenceforth the might of her advocacy was honoured by ever more fervent adoration. It came to be accepted, by Thomas Aquinas amongst others, that she was the 'Queen of Pity, as Christ was the King of Justice' and, in representations of the Last Judgement, she is sometimes seen thwarting the powers of Hell by pressing down with her finger the scale in which a human soul is precariously balanced against the weight of its misdeeds.

Many incidents drawn from the life and miracles of St. Mary are illustrated in English churches. Of the non-scriptural scenes, one that quite often appears is the Virgin, as a child, being taught to read by St. Anne. More frequently the Assumption and

[1] To be found in the *Protevangelium of James*, translated by M. R. James in *The Apocryphal New Testament*, pp. 38–49.

the Coronation of the Virgin are shown. According to a tradition which seems to have arisen in heretical circles during the fourth century, St. Mary was warned by Michael the Archangel of her approaching death, which took place in the presence of all the Apostles, who had been miraculously conveyed to Jerusalem. Her soul departed to Paradise, while her body was laid in a new tomb in the valley of Jehoshaphat, whence it was raised up by angels after three days and rejoined her soul. The Virgin was then crowned by Christ and enthroned as Queen of Heaven. Her usual emblem is the lily, the flower of purity; her badge is a capital M with a crown over it.

MARY MAGDALENE

Mary Magdalene (i.e. Mary of Magdala, a village near the sea of Galilee) is mentioned by St. Luke[1] as one of several women whom Jesus 'healed of evil spirits and infirmities'. She is not mentioned again in the Gospel story until the Crucifixion, when she stands among the many women who were then 'beholding from afar'[2] after following Jesus from Galilee and ministering to him. She was also a favoured witness of the Resurrection.[3] An unsolved question, which has exercised the minds of Biblical commentators from the second century until the present day, is whether Mary Magdalene is the same person as Mary of Bethany, the sister of Lazarus and Martha,[4] and as the unnamed woman also 'who was a sinner' and who, according to St. Luke,[5] approached Jesus in penitence when he was sitting at meat in a Pharisee's house and 'standing behind at his feet, weeping, began to wet his feet with her tears, and wiped them with the hair of her head, and kissed his feet and anointed them with ointment'. In the East these three Maries have been kept distinct, but in the West, at any rate since the time of St. Gregory the Great (d. A.D. 604), they have been identified. St. Mary

---

[1] viii. 2. [2] St. Mark xv. 40.
[3] St. Matthew xxviii; St. John xx.
[4] St. Luke x. 38–42; St. John xi. 1–45. [5] vii. 37–50.

Magdalene is therefore regularly represented as the type of the Christian penitent, with flowing hair, and holding her ointment-pot. Early traditions held that she died, perhaps as a martyr, at Ephesus, but this sober record was superseded by a more dramatic narrative, first found in the ninth century. According to this story, Mary Magdalene, Martha, Lazarus, and a number of other Christians were taken out to sea by their enemies in a rudderless ship, so that they might be drowned. The ship, however, came to land at Marseilles. There Lazarus became bishop, but Mary Magdalene, after a period of mission-preaching, left her companions and spent the last thirty years of her life in solitary contemplation near Aix-en-Provence.

MARY OF CLOPAS

One of the women who followed Jesus from Galilee. She is mentioned in St. John's Gospel[1] only, but is doubtless to be identified with 'Mary the mother of James the Less and of Joses'.[2] It is uncertain whether the expression 'Mary of Clopas' means that she was wife or daughter of Clopas, but in ecclesiastical tradition all became clear. She was held to be the daughter of Clopas (who had been St. Anne's second husband) and thus the half-sister of St. Mary the Virgin. She married Alphaeus, and was the mother of James, Joses, Simon, and Jude. On two Norfolk rood-screens[3] and in a few medieval windows she is depicted together with her four sons, each of whom bears his appropriate emblem.

[1] xix. 25.
[2] St. Mark xv. 40; St. Matthew xxvii. 56; St. Luke xxiv. 10.
[3] Ranworth and Houghton-le-dale.

MARY OF EGYPT

Mary of Egypt seems to be an unhistorical personage. She was said to have gone to Alexandria at the age of twelve and to have lived there as a prostitute until impelled by curiosity to join a pilgrimage to Jerusalem. Here she was prevented by a mysterious force from entering the church of the Holy Sepulchre 'for to worship the holy cross with the others'[1] and, being converted by this miracle, she resolved to spend the rest of her days in solitude and penitence. She retired beyond Jordan and lived in the desert without seeing another human being for seventeen years. At the end of that time a pious monk named Zosimus chanced upon her, was told her story, and undertook to return a year later with the Holy Sacrament. St. Mary of Egypt received the Sacrament with great devotion and died shortly afterwards. She is seldom shown in English churches, but may appear, as at Kenn, Devon, enveloped in long white hair and holding the three loaves which, together with such herbs as she could find, were her only sustenance in the wilderness.

[1] *Golden Legend*, iii. 107.

MARY SALOME

Salome is mentioned by St. Mark[1] as one of the women present at the Crucifixion and as afterwards bearing spices to the Sepulchre, and a comparison with St. Matthew's narrative[2] makes it apparent that she is to be identified with the mother of James and John, the sons of Zebedee. The later and variable traditions of the 'Three Maries' link Mary Salome with Mary Clopas and Mary Magdalene as early missioners of Provence or Spain. But no emblem derived from such stories is assigned to Salome in England. When she is represented, as on the screen at Ranworth, Norfolk, she is distinguished only by the presence of her two sons.

[1] xv. 40; xvi. 1. [2] xxvii. 56.

MATTHEW

While a customs-officer in the service of Herod Antipas, he was called to abandon his profession and become one of the Twelve Apostles.[1] He is to be identified with the Levi who 'made a great feast in his house', by attending which Jesus and his disciples scandalized the Pharisees.[2] According to the historian Eusebius,[3] Matthew preached 'to the Hebrews' and then, deciding to travel farther onwards, wrote a Gospel to leave with them. Later, unreliable traditions told of remarkably successful mission-preaching, accompanied by miraculous portents, in Ethiopia, where Matthew was said to have met his death by the sword for opposing a king's desire to marry a princess who had become a consecrated virgin. His emblem may therefore be a sword, but more often it is a money-box or money-bag. Sometimes he is confused with St. Matthias and bears an axe. Or he may hold a carpenter's square. St. Matthew, like the other evangelists, also has a symbol drawn from the imagery of Revelation iv. 7. Of the 'four living creatures full of eyes before and behind' to him is assigned the one that 'had a face as of a man'—usually represented as an angel under the influence of the first chapter of St. Matthew's Gospel in which an angel appears to Joseph in a dream.

[1] St. Matthew ix. 9.
[2] St. Mark ii. 14–17; St. Luke v. 27–32.
[3] *Ecclesiastical History*, iii. 24. 6.

MATTHIAS

One of Christ's earliest disciples, he was chosen by
lot to fill the vacant place among the Twelve Apostles
after the defection and death of Judas.[1] Nothing
certain is known about his missionary labours or the
manner of his death, but at Trèves, whither his relics
were brought, it was related that, after working
miraculous cures at Jerusalem, he was arrested by the
Jews, stoned, and finally beheaded with an axe. St.
Matthias therefore usually bears an axe or halberd,
but his emblem is variable and may be a sword or a
scimitar.

[1] Acts i. 21–6.

MAURICE

According to a fifth-century tradition that is repeated, with embellishments, in the *Golden Legend*, Maurice was the officer commanding a legion of 6,666 Christian knights drawn from Thebes, in Upper Egypt. This legion joined the army of the emperor Maximian which was led across the Alps on an expedition into Gaul about A.D. 290. At Agaunum (St. Moritz) the emperor ordered a general sacrifice to the gods of Rome and, when the Christians refused to participate, they were twice punished by the execution of every tenth man. Since they nevertheless remained firm in their resolve, the order was given that all should be put to death for insubordination, and they suffered martyrdom without attempting to offer resistance. St. Maurice is represented as a knight in armour, holding a banner or an axe.

MAURUS

Maurus (Maur) was educated at Subiaco where, in obedience to St. Benedict's command, he found himself empowered to walk on the water and thus save a fellow pupil, St. Placidus, from drowning. He accompanied St. Benedict to Monte Cassino whence he was sent with four companions to assist the bishop of Le Mans by establishing a monastery in his diocese (A.D. 543). The bishop died suddenly and his successor gave a hostile reception to the five Benedictines, but they enjoyed the patronage of Kings Theodebert and Clotaire I and founded the influential monastery of Glanfeuil for a hundred and forty monks. St. Maur, who gained some repute for healing a blind beggar and other sick persons, died in A.D. 584. In English churches, as on the rood-screen at Wolborough, Devon, he bears no distinctive emblem but appears as an abbot with book and crozier.

MAXENTIUS

Maxentius (about A.D. 440–515) is honoured with a church dedication at Bradshaw, Lancashire. He was abbot of a monastery near Poitiers and gained a local reputation as a wonder-worker. It is recorded that, when an army of Visigoths was ravaging his district, he calmly advanced to meet the barbarians. The arm of a soldier who raised his sword to strike the abbot was withered and afterwards, when the soldier expressed penitence, made whole again, whereat the Visigoths were filled with awe and left Maxentius' monastery unharmed.

MEDARD

Medard became bishop of Noyon in 531 and, from the next year, bishop of Tournai also. He was famous for missionary zeal and for extraordinary powers of curing disease, but suffered much vexation from King Clotaire I and the Frankish nobles. In spite of their violent opposition he yielded to the entreaties of Queen Radegund, bestowed the veil upon her, and ordained her a deaconess. When he died, about A.D. 545, his body was taken to Soissons, where a great abbey was built in his honour. Representations of St. Medard are very rare in English churches. At Wiggenhall St. Mary Magdalene, Norfolk, he is shown as a bishop holding a short sword, point upwards, in his right hand.

MELLITUS

Mellitus, a Roman abbot, was sent with a few companions by Pope Gregory the Great to reinforce St. Augustine's mission in England (A.D. 601). He was soon consecrated first bishop of London and, according to Bede,[1] the East Saxons 'received the word of truth by the preaching of Mellitus'. St. Paul's Cathedral was built, but in 616, after the death of the Christian kings Ethelbert and Sebert, Mellitus was banished and never recovered his see. On the conversion of King Eadbald, Mellitus was allowed to return to England, and he became archbishop of Canterbury in 619. He is said to have 'ruled the church of the English' with painstaking zeal in spite of suffering severely from gout and, on the occasion of an outbreak of fire at Canterbury, the fervour of his prayers brought about a change in the direction of the wind and averted much destruction. Mellitus was held in respect during the Middle Ages because of a tradition that connected him with the founding of Westminster Abbey and he is probably the bishop who is portrayed in a fourteenth-century window of the sanctuary at the Abbey.

[1] *Ecclesiastical History*, i. 3.

MICHAEL

To this much-loved angelic patron some 690 English churches were dedicated in the Middle Ages. In one of Daniel's visions[1] Michael was declared to be 'the great prince which standeth for the children of the people', that is, the guardian-angel of the Jews, who strove on behalf of his people against those spiritual powers which favoured Persia, and in the later Jewish literature he not seldom appears as 'one of the holy angels who has been ordained to protect the faithful among the people'.[2] So, in the Epistle of St. Jude,[3] reference is made to the legend that Michael the 'archangel' defended the body of Moses against the Devil who claimed it on the ground that Moses had been guilty of murdering an Egyptian. And, in the Revelation of St. John,[4] Michael appears as head of the angelic band which goes forth to war with the 'dragon' and his angels—'and the great dragon was cast down, the old serpent, he that is called the Devil and Satan, the deceiver of the whole world; he was cast down to the earth, and his angels were cast down with him'. St. Michael was thus the recognized leader of the spiritual forces contending for the Church against

---

[1] Daniel x. 13. 21; xii. 1.
[2] First Book of Enoch xx. 5.
[3] Verse 9.   [4] xii. 7.

the powers of darkness, in the certainty of ultimate triumph, and is often represented, in Christian art, as a winged angel, clad in armour and striking down the dragon which symbolizes the powers of evil. But what was also popularly remembered and illustrated was Michael's role in connexion with the judgement of souls, which he is seen weighing in the scales of justice before each one is assigned to its appropriate doom.

MILBURGA

Daughter of Merewald, king of Western Mercia, she built a nunnery at Much Wenlock and was consecrated as its first abbess. She is said to have escaped the attentions of an importunate suitor through the sudden rising of the river Corve, and it is claimed for her, as for St. Bridget and others, that she was able to hang up her veil on a sunbeam. But her best-remembered miracle was that some troublesome geese which were damaging her crops at Wenlock were driven away by her prayers and never dared return. St. Milburga therefore receives a goose as her emblem. She died about A.D. 722 and miracles of healing, such as were attributed to her during her lifetime, continued later on to be wrought by her relics.

MILDRED

Mildred was the daughter of King Merewald and sister of St. Milburga. According to her legend, she was sent by her mother to France, to be educated at the abbey of Chelles, but, when she declined to marry a relative of the abbess, she was subjected to malicious treatment and even shut up in a furnace. However, her life was miraculously preserved and she escaped by sea, bringing with her a number of relics and, in particular, a nail from the Cross. After landing at Ebbsfleet, she proceeded to Minster, in Thanet, where she succeeded Eormenburga as abbess (about A.D. 690) and earned widespread repute as one whose patient sanctity of life was able to overcome repeated onslaughts of the Devil. The stone on which she stepped as she landed in Kent took the impress of her foot and became a celebrated place of pilgrimage.

MODWENNA

Modwenna, abbess of a community of nuns in Armagh, sought the protection of King Aldfrid of Northumbria when her convent had been laid waste by raiders, about A.D. 700. Her history thereafter becomes subject to uncertain traditions, but she seems to have established another religious house near Burton-on-Trent, where an ancient church-dedication commemorates her.

MONNICA

Monnica serves as the pattern of a devout wife and mother. After her marriage to Patricius, a citizen of Tagaste in North Africa, she had to endure much rough, though not malicious, treatment, but, remaining submissive and ruling her house with diligence, she finally had the satisfaction of converting her husband to Christianity. She bore several children and, appreciating the unusual gifts of her son Augustine, watched over his intellectual and spiritual development with anxious care. She accompanied him to Milan, where she became a devoted supporter of St. Ambrose, and, just as Augustine's early waywardness had caused her bitter disappointment and grief, so she was filled with exultant joy at the news of his conversion. Shortly afterwards, when about to return to Africa, she fell ill and, having declared that her life work was accomplished, died in serene contentment. St. Monnica enjoyed little regard in medieval England, but her name has been included in the calendar of the 1928 Prayer Book.

NEOT

A monk of Glastonbury Abbey who had a share in the education of his kinsman, King Alfred. He retired to Hamstoke (now St. Neot), near Liskeard, where he lived as a hermit, but, after making a pilgrimage to Rome, he decided to adopt a more active way of life. He established and presided over a college of priests at Hamstoke, besides showing zeal in the evangelization of Cornwall. The most famous of the miracles connected with St. Neot is the story that, when his oxen were stolen, stags came out of the forest to take their place and willingly accepted the yoke, retiring at nightfall to the forest and returning each day until the thieves, penitent and amazed, brought the oxen back. St. Neot died about A.D. 877 and, less than a century later, his relics were seized, with the connivance of King Edgar, and transferred to St. Neots, Huntingdonshire, to enrich a newly founded priory. A medieval window at St. Neot, Cornwall, illustrates his life.

NICHOLAS

Bishop of Myra, in Asia Minor, during the first half of the fourth century A.D. He is said to have been present at the Council of Nicaea (325) and a church was dedicated to him at Constantinople about two centuries later by the emperor Justinian, but he is a shadowy figure. His *Life* consists mainly of a string of edifying acts of charity and spectacular miracles which testify rather to the creative imagination than to the historical accuracy of the biographer. Thus, he is said to have answered the prayer of some storm-tossed sailors and, joining them in their boat, to have quieted the fury of the seas: appearing in a dream to the emperor Constantine he induced him to pardon three innocent 'princes' who were in prison and awaiting execution: he provided wheat for his country during a famine by persuading the crews of Alexandrian ships to unload some of the grain on the understanding that, when they reached their destination, they would find their cargo undiminished: he restored to life three boys who, during another famine, had been cut up and thrown into a pickling-tub by an innkeeper who had no other meat to set before his guests. These and other marvels made him a most popular patron and about 400 churches in England are dedicated to him, but representations of him are comparatively rare.[1] He occasionally appears as a bishop, accompanied by the three boys in a pickling-tub, or with a ship. But his best-known emblem is to be seen suspended over pawnbrokers' shops. For St. Nicholas was patron saint of pawnbrokers, who adopted the sign of the three golden balls commemorating the three bags of gold which Nicholas left by stealth, one after another, in the house of an impoverished nobleman, that they might serve as dowries for his three daughters.

[1] Windows at Hillesden, Buckinghamshire, and North Moreton, Berkshire, illustrate his miracles.

NICOMEDE

Nicomede finds a place in the calendar[1] of the Anglican Prayer Book, but the details of his life are quite uncertain. He suffered martyrdom at Rome, and an apocryphal tradition records that he was a priest who was arrested and beaten to death in A.D. 81, for giving Christian burial to a certain Felicula, who had been savagely murdered by an enraged suitor when she expressed a preference for a life of virginity.

[1] 1 June.

NINIAN

Ninian was the first Christian missionary to visit Scotland. His *Life*, which is based on information given by Bede,[1] records that he was of royal birth and came from the district of Solway. After spending some years in study at Rome he was ordained bishop about A.D. 395 by Pope Siricius and sent back to Britain to evangelize the barbarous and remote districts beyond the Roman Wall. On his way thither he visited St. Martin at Tours and received from him capable stonemasons. These men built a noble church at Whitherne, on the coast of Wigtownshire, and here a monastic school was established which became a centre of Christian learning. St. Ninian died at Whitherne about A.D. 432. He is seldom depicted in English churches, but a statue in Worcester Cathedral of a bishop with a chain hanging over his right arm is probably intended to represent him.

[1] *Ecclesiastical History*, iii. 4.

ODO

Odo was of Danish parentage but became a keen supporter of the Anglo-Saxons as well as a convert to Christianity. He was a favourite at the court of King Athelstan and was appointed bishop of Wilton, being promoted in 942 to the archbishopric of Canterbury. Odo then took the habit of a Benedictine monk and began the policy, which his successor Dunstan carried more fully into effect, of enforcing strict discipline upon monks and secular clergy alike. Odo was little regarded in the Middle Ages, but he appears, in a fifteenth-century window at All Souls College, Oxford, vested as an archbishop, holding book and cross.

OLAVE

Olave was king of Norway, A.D. 1015–30. An adventurous autocrat who spared neither himself nor anyone else in his attempts to secure national unity, he was enthusiastic in his support of Christianity in Scandinavia and vigorous in repressing any revivals of paganism, offering to his subjects the alternative 'Be baptized or fight'. His uncompromising severity caused a rebellion and he had to flee to Russia, but he returned a year later at the head of a large army and fell in battle near Trondhjem. St. Olave is shown as a king holding a battle-axe. Occasionally, as on the screen at Barton Turf, Norfolk, he has loaves of bread as well. This commemorates no incident in his life, but is a pun on the Latin version of his name— Holofius—which suggested a 'whole loaf' to the artist.

OSMUND

Osmund, a nephew of William the Conqueror, gained renown from his early years for piety and asceticism. After a period of study at Paris he was employed by the king in high offices of state and helped to compile Domesday Book, but in 1078 he abandoned his secular career and was consecrated bishop of Salisbury. Active both as scholar and as administrator, he completed the building of the Cathedral at Old Sarum and enriched it with a splendid library, as well as working out its constitutions so carefully that they came to be regarded as a model. Moreover his revision of the liturgy resulted in the 'Sarum Use', or Cathedral service-book, which was widely adopted in other dioceses and underlies the present Book of Common Prayer. St. Osmund died in A.D. 1099. Three churches in Dorset are dedicated to him, and he is occasionally portrayed, in medieval glass, as a bishop without distinctive emblem.

OSWALD

King of Northumbria, A.D. 634–42. He was the son
of King Ethelfrid but, after his father's death, sought
refuge in Scotland and was converted to Christianity
by the monks of Iona. However, after seventeen
years of exile, he recovered his ancestral domain by
defeating the British chieftain Caedwalla at the battle
of Heavenfield. Before combat was joined, the king
and his troops knelt in prayer around a hastily erected
wooden cross which was afterwards believed to possess miraculous powers. Oswald added wide terri-
tories to his realm and thus incurred the enmity of
Penda, king of Mercia, but his chief interest lay in the
arts of peace and particularly in the diffusion of the
Christian faith. He was the active patron and close
friend of St. Aidan who was sent from Iona to preach
the Gospel in Northumbria, and he persuaded Cynegils, king of Wessex, whose daughter he married, to
be baptized and to establish the bishopric of Dorchester (Oxfordshire). His charitable disposition is
illustrated by the story that one Easter Day, when he
and Aidan were dining together, he learned that a
crowd of beggars had assembled outside the hall in
the hope of securing some scraps. Oswald, leaving
untasted the dainty food that had just been set in a
silver dish before him, ordered that not only should
the food be divided amongst the beggars but that
the dish also should be broken in pieces and distri-
buted. St. Oswald met his death at the battle of
Maserfield, when fighting against King Penda. He
is represented as a king with sceptre and cross but
he may, as at Wells Cathedral, hold a silver dish.

Medieval craftsmen sometimes show St. Cuthbert holding the crowned head of St. Oswald, since the head was taken to Lindisfarne for burial and then, in A.D. 875 when the Danish invasions threatened, was placed in St. Cuthbert's coffin and transferred eventually to Durham.

OSWIN

Oswin was a kinsman of Oswy, who succeeded his brother St. Oswald on the throne of Northumbria in A.D. 642. After Oswald's death Oswin returned to Deira (Yorkshire), which had for a short time been under the rule of his father Osric, and was acclaimed as king by the people who desired to be independent of Oswy. According to Bede,[1] Oswin combined attractiveness of manner and person with humble piety, and he gave every encouragement to the missionary endeavours of St. Aidan. But he aroused the jealousy of Oswy, who lamented the division of the kingdom of Northumbria, and when, declining an unequal battle, he retired to the house of his friend, Count Hunwald, at Gilling, he was betrayed by Hunwald and murdered. The monks of Tynemouth priory later claimed to possess his relics and on the priory seal, as occasionally elsewhere, St. Oswin appears as a king holding a spear.

[1] *Ecclesiastical History*, iii. 14.

OSYTH

Her legendary *Life* records that she was a seventh-century princess of Mercia who, much against her will, was assigned as wife to King Sighere of the East Saxons. When she ran away from her husband and took the veil, Sighere acquiesced and bestowed on her an estate at Chick, Essex, where she built a nunnery and became its first abbess. But some Danish pirates sacked the nunnery and decapitated St. Osyth, who walked away to the nearest church carrying her own head. She is therefore represented holding her head in her hands.

OUEN

Ouen or Audoenus (A.D. 610–83) was attached to the Frankish court and rose to the rank of Chancellor under King Dagobert. But, influenced by St. Eloi, he sought a monastic life and founded the abbey of Rebais, whence he was summoned to become bishop of Rouen. During his long episcopate, which lasted over forty years, he gained renown for his humble piety, and showed both courage and political good sense in the advice and support which he gave to Queen Bathildis when she was left a young widow in 657, and to her son, the boy king Clotaire III. St. Ouen travelled widely on religious and diplomatic missions, and the ending of a seven-year drought in Spain was ascribed to the efficacy of his prayers.

PANCRAS

A martyr at Rome about A.D. 305. His unreliable legend relates that he came, together with his uncle Dionysius, from Phrygia to Rome, where they were both converted to Christianity. Pancras attracted the favourable notice of Diocletian but, although only fourteen years old, he refused to yield either to threats or to blandishments when the emperor urged him to renounce his faith, and was therefore beheaded. His shrine at Rome became famous as a place where solemn oaths were taken, since no perjury could be committed there with impunity. The first church at Canterbury was dedicated by St. Augustine to the honour of St. Pancras, and his cult in England became popular when some of his relics were presented by Pope Vitalian to King Oswy. St. Pancras is not often represented by medieval artists, but he may appear as a youth with sword or palm-branch and book. Occasionally he holds a stone, but is then to be identified with a different St. Pancras who, according to a very dubious tradition, was consecrated by St. Peter as first bishop of Taormina, in Sicily, and stoned to death by infuriated pagans.

PANDIANA

Pandiana, an Irish princess, received such harsh treatment at home that she fled for protection to Eltisley, in Cambridgeshire, where a relative was prioress of the nunnery. Here she lived a life of quiet sanctity, and the church at Eltisley is dedicated to her memory.

PATRICK

Patrick, the apostle and patron of Ireland, is the subject of confused and often fanciful traditions, but that he was a courageous and successful missionary in Ireland during the fifth century cannot be doubted. He seems to have been born in Dumbartonshire, but was taken captive by raiders and became the slave of Milchu, a chieftain in Antrim. Six years later he escaped to Gaul and pursued a long course of study under the direction of such scholars as St. Germanus of Auxerre. But his evangelistic zeal and knowledge of Celtic customs and language naturally led to his return to Ireland. After several reverses he reached the Hill of Slane, where he challenged King Loigaire by kindling the Paschal fire on Easter Eve, which happened also to be the occasion of a pagan festival. Loigaire marched against him, but succumbed to the charm of his sincerity and the logical clarity of his preaching, which was helped by such illustrations as the three-leaved shamrock held forward to demonstrate the Trinity. Thereafter St. Patrick travelled widely throughout Ireland, establishing churches and, according to some accounts, performing such works of mercy as the expulsion of all snakes and poisonous animals from the island by the help of a staff which he claimed to have received as the gift of Christ. St. Patrick died about A.D. 463 and was buried at Saul, in County Down. Though he has half a dozen ancient churches dedicated to him in England, he was neglected by the English artists of the Middle Ages and is rarely depicted with the snakes that are his characteristic emblem.

PAUL

The story of St. Paul's conversion and heroic missionary labours, as related in the Acts of the Apostles, was dramatic enough to need no further enrichment. But Acts finishes with the statement that Paul 'abode two whole years in his own hired dwelling' at Rome 'preaching the kingdom of God and teaching the things concerning the Lord Jesus Christ with all boldness, none forbidding him'. Supplementing this account, the tradition soon came to be accepted that Paul left Rome in order to carry out further evangelization particularly in Spain, a country which he had long desired to visit. After several years of travel he returned to Rome, where his influence was such that many quite eminent persons were converted. The emperor Nero became apprehensive that those who accepted Christ as their king might prove disloyal to himself, and so gave orders for Paul to be beheaded. The Apostle of the Gentiles therefore bears the sword as his regular emblem. In ecclesiastical art, as in church dedications, he is often linked with St. Peter, and this association may be traced back as far as the closing years of the first century when, in the letter from the Christians of Rome to those of Corinth which goes by the name of the First Epistle of Clement, the Corinthians are reminded: 'Through jealousy and envy the greatest and most righteous pillars were persecuted and strove unto death. Let us set before our eyes the good apostles. Peter, who because of unrighteous jealousy endured not one or two but many trials and after thus giving his testimony went to the place of glory which was his due.

Through jealousy and strife Paul marked out the path to the prize of endurance: seven times was he in bonds, he suffered exile, he was stoned, he became a herald both in the East and in the West, he gained noble fame for his faith, he taught righteousness to the whole world, and, after he had come to the limits of the West and given his testimony before the rulers, he thus departed from the world and was taken up into the holy place.'[1]

[1] 1 Clement v. The text is given in the Loeb edition of the *Apostolic Fathers*, volume i.

PAUL OF THEBES

Paul of Thebes is described by St. Jerome[1] as the 'founder of the monastic life'. He is said to have retired, when still a boy, to the Egyptian desert in horror at the persecution of the emperor Decius (about A.D. 250) and to have passed nearly a hundred years in solitary asceticism. Shortly before his death he was visited and reverenced by St. Antony, who obtained his coat, made from palm-leaves, and wore it at great festivals. St. Paul of Thebes is rarely depicted, but he may be shown, as at Wolborough, Devon, with the raven which brought him half a loaf for his sustenance every day.

[1] Letter xxii. 36.

PAULINUS

Paulinus was one of a small band of missionaries sent by Pope Gregory I in A.D. 601 to help St. Augustine in his task of evangelizing England. When Ethelburga, daughter of King Ethelbert of Kent, departed for Northumbria to marry the pagan King Edwin, Paulinus accompanied her as chaplain-bishop. He preached and taught with great vigour, and Bede mentions the baptism of numerous converts in the Swale, Derwent, and Trent as well as in the streams of Northumbria and at Lincoln. In 627 Edwin himself accepted the Faith but, six years later, the king was defeated and slain by Penda of Mercia at the battle of Heathfield, and Ethelburga returned to Kent. Paulinus came with her and was appointed bishop of Rochester, where he remained until his death in 644.

PEGA

Pega was the sister of St. Guthlac and followed his example by dedicating herself to the monastic life. She founded a small community at Peakirk, on the edge of the Lincolnshire Fens in which Guthlac dwelt, but paid no visit to Crowland until she went there to attend her brother's burial. Thereafter she became more rigorous in her self-inflicted mortifications and died, when on a pilgrimage to Rome, about A.D. 717. The church at Peakirk (Pega's Kirk) is dedicated to her.

PELAGIUS

After gaining high regard at the court of the emperor Justinian, he returned to Rome and was appointed archdeacon. He became renowned for charity and benevolence, and was successful in persuading King Totila to spare the city when the Goths captured it. Pelagius was consecrated pope in A.D. 555, but his five years of office were uneasy, since he became involved in political intrigues and his orthodoxy was challenged. A window in the ante-chapel at New College, Oxford, shows him as a pope, wearing the tiara.

PERPETUA

Perpetua suffered martyrdom at Carthage in A.D. 203. An edict of the emperor Septimius Severus had forbidden any fresh conversions to Christianity, so that Perpetua and several of her friends, who were receiving instruction with a view to baptism, were arrested. The *Acts of St. Perpetua*, an obviously genuine document, record her constancy both in rejecting the appeals of her distracted father that she should participate in the formal sacrifices of paganism and in enduring the rigours of imprisonment which, however, were mitigated by a series of consoling visions. St. Perpetua and her companions, after impressing all spectators by their calm and confident bearing, met their death in the amphitheatre; Perpetua being first gored by a wild cow and then dispatched with the sword. Though her feast-day, 7 March, is noted in the Anglican calendar, St. Perpetua failed to find favour in England as a patron saint.

PETER

In spite of the impetuous[1] and even inconstant[2] elements in his character, Peter was one of the three privileged Apostles who accompanied Jesus on such solemn occasions as the Transfiguration and the Agony in Gethsemane.[3]   The promise[4] 'Thou art Peter, and upon this rock I will build my Church, and the gates of Hades shall not prevail against it: I will give unto thee the keys of the kingdom of Heaven' has, from an early date, been taken to imply that Peter was to enjoy a position of pre-eminence in the New Israel. The early chapters of the Acts of the Apostles indicate that he did in fact exercise authority at first over the Christian community, but by the time of the Council of Jerusalem[5] (about A.D. 49) St. James has become president of the Church and St. Peter thereafter disappears from the narrative of Acts. Some support may, however, be drawn, from the writings of Origen and others, for the view that Peter, after organizing and presiding over the church at Antioch, proceeded to Rome, where he became bishop and suffered together with St. Paul in the Neronian persecution of A.D. 64. He is said to have been crucified head downwards, in deference to his plea that he was 'not worthy to be put on the cross like as his Lord was'. St. Peter's emblem is nearly always a key or keys, but he may

---

[1] St. Mark viii. 32-3.   [2] St. Luke xxii. 33-4.
[3] St. Matthew xxvi. 36-46.   [4] St. Matthew xvi. 18.
[5] Acts xv.

have a chain instead. This alludes to his release by
the angel from the prison in which he had been cast
by Herod Agrippa I,[1] an incident in the Apostle's life
which is commemorated by the festival of St. Peter's
Chains.[2]

[1] Acts xii.
[2] 1 Aug. in the West; 16 Jan. in the Greek Church.

PETER THE EXORCIST

Peter the Exorcist was commemorated at Rome as
one of the most notable martyrs who suffered in
Diocletian's persecution (about A.D. 303), and it was
recorded that, whilst in prison and awaiting execution, he demonstrated the power of Christianity by
repeatedly breaking his bonds and by freeing the
jailer's daughter from demonic possession. Over his
tomb the emperor Constantine built a church
wherein St. Helen was buried. He gained little regard in England, but is shown in glass that dates
from the reign of Henry VIII at Winscombe,
Somerset.

PETER MARTYR

Peter Martyr (Peter of Milan) was a native of Verona who studied at the university of Bologna and became a Dominican friar. In 1234 he was sent as inquisitor to purge northern Italy of heresy, a task for which he was well fitted by reason of his zeal, his powerful eloquence, and a reputation as a worker of miracles. But the times were troubled owing to the prolonged warfare between Pope Innocent IV and the emperors Frederick II and Conrad IV, so that opportunity was easily found by the heretics to exact their revenge. The inquisitor was waylaid near Milan by two hired assassins who cleft open his head with the blow of an axe and then stabbed him to the heart (A.D. 1252). Therefore when Peter Martyr appears in English churches, as on the rood-screen at Hennock, Devonshire, he has a knife fixed in his head. Or he may hold a cutlass and a book.

PETROCK

Thirteen churches, all in Devon and Cornwall, are dedicated to this saint, but the details of his life are obscure. He seems to have sailed from Wales or Ireland to the coast of Cornwall in the seventh century and, after landing at Padstow, to have settled in a hermitage at Bodmin where his relics were later venerated. His reputation for sanctity caused others to join him and the hermitage developed into a monastic college.

PETRONILLA

An inscription found in a Christian cemetery on the Ardeatine Way at Rome, but now destroyed, used with brief simplicity to commemorate 'Aurelia Petronilla, a much-loved daughter'. This Petronilla was probably a member of the family of the Flavii who owned the cemetery and were the descendants of one Petronius; but a misunderstanding of the inscription may lie behind the apocryphal story of Petronilla which appears, in its fully developed form, in the fifth century. According to this legend, she was a daughter of St. Peter and suffered from paralysis. Peter was one day rebuked for failing to use his miraculous powers to cure his daughter, whereat, after explaining that the sickness was for her good, he promised that she should recover for a short while and wait upon the company. Petronilla did so, but immediately afterwards was again afflicted by her malady and returned to bed. In due time she was restored to health, and then her beauty so attracted a certain count Flaccus that he came, supported by an armed band, to persuade or else to force her into marriage with him. She begged for a delay of three days, during which she gave herself up to prayer and fasting, and when Flaccus arrived to claim his bride he found that in fulfilment of her dearest wish she had died. Because of her connexion with St. Peter, Petronilla holds a key, or key and book, as her emblem.

PHILIP

Philip appears as an Apostle in all the Gospels, but no details of his life are given except by St. John. A native of Bethsaida in Galilee, he seems to have received his call to follow Jesus whilst he was one of the crowd of people attracted to 'Bethany beyond Jordan' by the preaching of John the Baptist.[1] He was present on the occasion of the feeding of the multitude, when he answered Jesus' inquiry, 'Whence are we to buy bread that these may eat?', by saying, 'Two hundred pennyworth of bread is not sufficient for them, that everyone may take a little';[2] he was accosted by 'certain Greeks' who had come up to Jerusalem to celebrate the Passover and wished to 'see Jesus',[3] and he is mentioned as interrupting Jesus' discourse at the Last Supper with the request, 'Lord, show us the Father and it sufficeth us.'[4] The subsequent history of St. Philip is obscure owing to the confusion between himself and Philip the Evangelist, whose appointment as one of the Seven Deacons and successful missionary labours in Samaria are recorded in the Acts of the Apostles.[5] But the tradition prevailed that, after a spell of itinerant preaching, he settled with two of his daughters at Hierapolis, in Asia Minor, where he was crucified

---

[1] St. John i. 43.   [2] St. John vi. 7.
[3] St. John xii. 21.   [4] St. John xiv. 8.
[5] Acts vi. 5; viii. 5–40; cf. xxi. 8.

at the age of eighty-seven by his pagan opponents. St. Philip has alternative emblems—a basket containing loaves, as suggested by the part he played in the feeding of the multitude, or a long cross, to commemorate the manner of his death.

PLACIDUS

Several unnamed figures of Benedictine monks in fifteenth-century church windows have been identified with St. Placidus, a favourite disciple and companion of St. Benedict. Little is known about him except the story that, shortly after he had been entrusted, at the age of seven, to Benedict's care, he fell into the lake at Subiaco from which he was miraculously rescued by another pupil, St. Maurus, who was empowered at Benedict's command to walk on the water. This St. Placidus is sometimes confused with a dubious namesake who is said to have been killed at Messina by some Saracen pirates because he refused to reverence their gods.

POLYCARP

Polycarp serves as an example of those early Fathers of the Church whose strenuous and beneficent lives were crowned by a martyr's death but who yet failed to achieve popularity as patrons in the Middle Ages. As a boy, Polycarp was instructed by St. John and by other disciples of Jesus, and his forty years as bishop of Smyrna were distinguished rather by his tenacious grasp on the truths he had learned than by speculation or novelty. When Ignatius, bishop of Antioch, was being taken as a prisoner to Rome, he wrote to Polycarp, 'the times have need of thee as pilots have need of winds . . . be thou therefore firm as an anvil when it is smitten', and all that is known of Polycarp's life indicates that he followed this advice and exercised a steadying influence on the Church in Asia during a period of stress and change. The manner of his death is known from an eyewitness account. The excitement caused at Smyrna by the ceremonies and games connected with the festival of the Community of Asia emboldened the Jews and other opponents to cry out for the death of Christians who declined to participate in the celebrations. Polycarp had retired to a small farm just outside the city and thence he was brought, under arrest, to answer a charge of 'atheism'. The proconsul and other officials strove hard to persuade him to renounce his Christianity but, since he remained unmoved either by threats or by entreaties and the popular tumult was increasing, he was taken away to be burnt at the stake. The flames seemed not to affect the body of the martyr but only to form a canopy of fire around him, so he was thrust through with a sword.[1] Polycarp is seldom depicted in English churches and has no characteristic emblem. In seventeenth-century glass at Magdalen College, Oxford, he is seen trampling on a pagan.

[1] The *Martyrdom of Polycarp* is printed in the Loeb edition of the Apostolic Fathers, volume ii.

PRISCA

Prisca the martyr is not the Prisca, or Priscilla, mentioned in the Acts of the Apostles and in the Second Epistle to Timothy, who, together with her husband Aquila, gave St. Paul a lodging at Corinth and accompanied him to Ephesus. Her legend makes her a Roman maiden who, in the reign of Claudius Gothicus (A.D. 268–70), was condemned to be torn to pieces by a lion in the amphitheatre. However, the king of beasts refused to do her any harm, and when she had been beheaded an eagle, king of birds, honoured her sanctity by keeping a vigil over her dead body. St. Prisca is commemorated in the Anglican calendar on 18 January, but failed to achieve popularity as a patron saint in England.

PROSDOCIMUS

Prosdocimus is honoured as the first bishop of Padua. His unhistorical *Acts* relate that he accompanied St. Peter to Rome whence he passed to Padua and evangelized the surrounding district. St. Prosdocimus, though little known in England, appears in a window at Wiggenhall St. Mary Magdalen, Norfolk, vested as a bishop, with right hand raised in blessing.

QUINTIN

Quintin is said to have been a Roman soldier who gave up his career in order to preach the Gospel in the region of Amiens, where he was arrested by order of 'Rictiovarus', representative of the emperor Maximian (A.D. 287). He remained 'constant and unmovable'[1] under fantastic tortures and was finally beheaded. St. Quintin gives his name to the town in north-eastern France where his uncorrupt body was discovered, many years after his death, as the result of a vision. His shrine gained renown for miracles of healing and he was invoked with particular success in cases of dropsy.

[1] *Golden Legend*, vi, p. 82.

RADEGUND

Radegund, a princess of Thuringia, was only a child when she was taken captive by the conquering Franks. By order of Clotaire I, who was attracted by her beauty, she received such an education as would fit her eventually to become his queen, and, in spite of the fact that she made no secret of her desire to live as a nun, she was compelled to marry the king when she reached the age of eighteen. After six miserable years in the uncongenial atmosphere of the Frankish Court, Radegund was emboldened, in a passion of anger and grief which she experienced on hearing that her much-loved brother had been put to death on Clotaire's orders, to demand her freedom. She fled to Noyon and was successful in persuading St. Medard to bestow the veil upon her and ordain her deaconess. Clotaire then behaved with magnanimity, and granted her land and money with which to establish a nunnery at Poitiers. Radegund refused the title of abbess, and aspired to a pre-eminence only in the rigour of her self-discipline and the fervour with which she carried out the humblest domestic duties or tended the most unattractive invalids. But she exercised such influence that her wishes were in fact accepted as binding by the other nuns, and, when she died in A.D. 587, she was mourned as their Mother in God. St. Radegund has no distinctive emblem. She may be shown as a royal abbess, crowned, and holding crozier and book.

REMIGIUS

Remigius gained such renown for his devout and unworldly life that, when the bishopric of Rheims became vacant, he was elected by popular acclamation to fill it, although he was only twenty-two years of age and a layman. Throughout his long episcopate, which is said to have lasted from A.D. 457 to 530, Remigius was distinguished for the eloquence of his preaching and for the vigour with which he strove to effect the conversion of the Franks to orthodox Christianity. The queen afforded him valuable support, but King Clovis was resolute in declining to be baptized. At last, however, when hard pressed in battle, Clovis promised that, if the God whom his wife worshipped gave him victory, he would serve Him alone. The king unexpectedly won the day and in fulfilment of his vow forthwith submitted to baptism at the hands of Remigius. The occasion was one of great splendour but, according to a widely received legend, the holy oils had not been prepared and a dove settled the bishop's perplexity by descending from heaven bearing a vessel that contained the necessary chrism. In continental glass Remigius is commonly shown with the dove that brought him the oil, but in England, although five ancient churches are dedicated to him, he was not a favourite subject with medieval artists.

RICHARD OF CHICHESTER

Richard de Wyche lost a comfortable home and was reduced to poverty by the untimely death of his parents. But, after working hard and to good effect on a farm belonging to his brother, he was able to indulge his natural bent for scholarship and studied law and logic with brilliant success in the universities of Paris, Oxford, and Bologna. He was appointed chancellor of Oxford and of Canterbury, but when his archbishop, St. Edmund of Abingdon, became involved in controversy with King Henry III and left the country, Richard de Wyche accompanied him to Pontigny. After Edmund's death Richard settled in a Dominican friary at Orléans, where he gained renown alike for his learning and for his vigorous asceticism. Returning to England in 1244 he was soon elected bishop of Chichester, but Henry III, infuriated at this elevation of an opponent, refused to hand over the temporalities of the see until induced to do so by a threat of excommunication from Pope Innocent IV. As a bishop Richard displayed self-denying generosity towards the poor coupled with a stern determination to enforce rigid discipline upon the clergy of his diocese. Careful regulations were drawn up to ensure that divine service was celebrated with seemliness and reverence, and great encouragement was offered to friars who wished to work in Sussex. Richard died at Dover in 1253, worn out by a long preaching tour in support of the Crusades. His shrine in Chichester Cathedral became a favourite place of pilgrimage, notable for miraculous cures, and his renown is proved by his inclusion in a very select band of saints whose pictures, painted before the end of the thirteenth century, adorn the Relic Chamber in Norwich Cathedral. St. Richard is shown as a bishop without distinctive emblem.

RICHARD SCROPE

Richard Scrope, after being chancellor of the University of Cambridge and bishop of Lichfield, was promoted in 1398 to the see of York. He transferred his loyalty from Richard II to Henry IV, but in 1404 made vigorous protests against the abuses which marked the beginning of Henry's reign. With the enthusiastic support of the citizens of York, Scrope joined Thomas Mowbray, the earl marshal, in leading an armed force against the royal troops who were pressing northwards under the command of the Earl of Westmorland. When Westmorland promised that he would try to persuade the king to consider the proposed reforms, Scrope caused his followers to disperse, whereat he was treacherously arrested and beheaded. His shrine, in the Lady Chapel of the Minster, became such a focus of Yorkshire patriotism that Henry's government ordered that it should be covered up with stones and timber to keep the people away. Though never formally canonized, he continued to receive honour as a saint and martyr. In a fifteenth-century window of the choir-transept at York Minster he is shown as an archbishop holding a cross-staff and wearing the pall.

RICHARIUS

Richarius (Riquier) is said to have been a young chieftain in the district of Abbeville, in Picardy, who was converted by two Irish missionaries early in the seventh century. He became fired with zeal to preach and to cure disease, and he resolved also to devote the greater part of his considerable possessions towards providing a ransom for prisoners. Under the patronage of King Dagobert I he established a monastery at Centule (now St-Riquier) and then, desiring to practise severer austerities, withdrew to a lonely hermitage in the forest where, however, he was often thronged by crowds of sick people desiring to benefit from his healing touch. He died about A.D. 645. St. Richarius seems to have made a missionary tour in England, and the church at Aberford, Yorkshire, is probably dedicated to him, but he failed to achieve popularity except in his own district of France.

ROBERT OF KNARESBOROUGH

Robert of Knaresborough, though never canonized, was much venerated in Yorkshire, and the church at Pannal is dedicated to him. The son of a Lord Mayor of York, Robert Flower gave up a life of affluence in order to spend his days as a hermit. At first he dwelt in a cell hewn out of the rock overhanging the River Nidd, but later he moved to a more luxurious establishment provided for him by a devout patroness. Here he dispensed a lavish charity and thus aroused the fears and the hostility of a powerful baron, William de Stuteville, who expelled Robert from the buildings and destroyed them. Robert returned to his cell by the Nidd and devoted himself to intercessory prayer. His fame attracted a number of visitors including King John, who received a cool welcome; and, after his death in 1218, his body was jealously guarded by the monks of Knaresborough Priory in the chapel which had been built by Robert's brother alongside the hermit-cell.

ROCH

Roch gained great popularity as a protector from plague, and the bishops assembled for the Council of Constance in 1414 approved his cult and held a procession in his honour. However, his *Life*, as it appears in the *Golden Legend*, is largely unhistorical. According to this account, Roch was a native of Montpellier who, in accordance with his father's dying wish, devoted himself and his possessions to the relief of the sick and poor. Clad in the habit of a pilgrim he proceeded to Acquapendente, in Italy, and caused an epidemic of plague to cease (about 1350). The same happy result was ascribed to his presence at Rome and elsewhere in Italy, but at Piacenza he himself caught the infection and was expelled from the city. He made a hut for himself in the woods and dwelt there until he was restored to health, while a dog brought him a loaf of bread each day from his master's table. Eventually Roch was arrested as a spy and died after five years of willingly accepted privations in prison. He is regularly shown as a pilgrim, pointing to a plague spot on his thigh.

ROMANUS

He was a favourite at the court of King Clotaire II of the Franks, gained repute for piety, and, amidst general acclamation, was appointed bishop of Rouen in A.D. 628. He showed great vigour in his efforts to exterminate all pagan practices in his diocese. St. Romanus is very rarely depicted in England; when he appears it is as a bishop with no distinctive emblem.

RUMBALD

Some of the seven English church dedications to St. Rumbald may be intended to honour St. Rumbold, an Irishman whose legendary *Life* makes him bishop of Mechlin in the eighth century, or even St. Romuald (952–1027), ascetic founder of the Order of Camaldolese Hermits. But more probably they all testify to the fame of the English St. Rumbald, infant son of a Northumbrian king and a princess of Mercia. According to a widespread legend, this remarkable child died when three days old, but not before he had openly declared 'I am a Christian', demanded baptism, and delivered a sermon. His birthplace is given as King's Sutton, Northamptonshire, near which village St. Rumbald's well is still to be seen.

SAMPSON

A dubious tradition, not clearly formulated until the twelfth century, tells of a St. Sampson, 'a man of great quality and much celebrated for his piety', who was summoned from Wales to act as bishop of York. More substantial is the figure of St. Sampson of Dol, who was present at the Council of Paris in A.D. 557 and appended his signature to the canons there approved. He, too, is said to have been a Welshman, remarkable for his austerities, who was consecrated bishop by St. Dubritius and then called upon by the people of Dol, in Brittany, to preside over their church. They were induced to make this choice partly because of his reputed power to restrain birds from attacking the crops. When St. Sampson is depicted, as in fifteenth-century glass at Wiggenhall St. Mary Magdalen, Norfolk, he appears as a bishop with no distinctive emblem.

SCHOLASTICA

Scholastica (about A.D. 480–542) was the sister of St. Benedict and she, too, felt the vocation to a monastic life. She dwelt first of all in a cell near Subiaco, but later, when her brother moved to Monte Cassino, she also migrated in order that she might enjoy occasional visits from him. She is traditionally described as an abbess, and it is as a Benedictine abbess that she is represented by medieval artists.

SEBASTIAN

Sebastian, one of the most famous of the Roman martyrs, is said to have been a favourite with Diocletian but to have been executed by the emperor's order for obstinate adherence to Christianity and for scorning the gods of Rome. He was tied to a stake and shot at by archers 'until he was as full of arrows as an urchin is full of pricks'.[1] Though left for dead, he was restored to health by the ministrations of a pious woman named Irene; but, when he reappeared in Rome,  he was again arrested and stoned by order of Diocletian. The traditional date of his death is A.D. 287. St. Sebastian enjoyed popularity in the Middle Ages as a patron against plague, the sudden onslaught of which is typified by an arrow. The mode of his death provided the reason for his fame and he is regularly shown, though not often in English churches, as a naked youth bound to a tree and pierced by arrows, or, occasionally, clothed and holding an arrow.

[1] *Golden Legend*, ii, p. 243.

SEXBURGA

Sexburga (about A.D. 620–99), one of the four saintly daughters of Anna, king of the East Angles, married Erconbert, king of Kent, who was renowned for his piety and for his resolute repression of pagan worship in his kingdom. After her husband's death Sexburga seems to have acted as regent, but she gladly handed over the government to her son Egbert when he came of age, and retired to the Isle of Sheppey, where she founded a monastic community. She later decided to return to East Anglia and join her sister St. Etheldreda at Ely and, when Etheldreda died, she was chosen as abbess and ruled over the monastery for twenty years.

SIDWELL

Sidwell (Sativola) was formerly held in high honour in
the west of England, but no
clear traditions of her life and
death remain beyond the fact
that she suffered martyrdom,
about A.D. 740, on the site of
St. Sidwell's Church, Exeter.
In that church, and on several
Devonshire rood-screens, she
is shown decapitated and bearing her head in her hands.[1]
Sometimes she holds a scythe
and stands near a well, and
these emblems may be no
more than a punning allusion

to her name, which was sometimes written Sithewell.
But local legend recorded that she was a maiden
whose reputation for piety became so widespread
that her stepmother was moved with jealousy and
bribed some haymakers to attack Sidwell with their
scythes. Where she fell dead a fountain immediately
sprang up and the choicest flowers bedecked the
earth all around.

[1] St. Sidwell's Church was largely destroyed by enemy action
in May 1942, but there is a carving of the saint, as described
in the text, on one of the pillars still standing. There is also
a good representation of her in the great east window of
Exeter Cathedral.

SIGFRID

Sigfrid (Siegfried), a priest of York, was sent out as a missionary bishop to preach the Faith in Norway when King Olaf Tryggvesson, after his acceptance of Christianity, appealed for help to King Ethelred II of England (about A.D. 995). Sigfrid travelled onwards into Sweden where his heroic labours resulted in the conversion and baptism of many of the inhabitants, including the king, and won back a considerable district which had lapsed into idolatry after the withdrawal of St. Anskar and his missionaries. Sigfrid is very rarely to be seen in English churches, but in a window of the choir at York Minster he is portrayed as a bishop with no distinctive emblem.

SILVESTER

Silvester, bishop of Rome A.D. 314–35, appears to have been a comparatively undistinguished pope, and few historical facts are known about him except that he occupied the see of Rome at an important time when imperial patronage was taking the place of imperial persecution and that he excused himself from attendance at the great Council of Nicaea (325) on the ground of old age. But a luxuriant crop of legend, derived from the apocryphal *Acts of St. Silvester*, gathered round his name and ensured his repute in the Middle Ages. He was said to have baptized Constantine and thus cured the emperor of leprosy which had fallen upon him as a punishment for cruel persecutions; again, he raised a dead bull to life in order to confound his Jewish opponents and overcame a pestilential dragon which, lurking in a pit near Rome, slew three hundred men a day with its breath. Representations of St. Silvester are very rare in England. When he appears, as at Houghton St. Giles, Norfolk, he is shown as a pope with tiara and double cross but lacking any distinctive emblem.

SIMON

Simon is numbered in the Gospels[1] and in Acts[2] as one of the Twelve Apostles, but nothing further is recorded about him. The name was a common one and Simon the Apostle was distinguished by the epithet 'Cananaean' or 'Zealot' to indicate that he had been a member of the sect established by the fiery Judas of Gamala who headed the militant opposition to the Roman authorities in Palestine. Simon was later identified with Simon the 'brother of the Lord',[3] who, according to ecclesiastical tradition derived from St. Jerome, was really a son of Mary, the wife of Cleopas, and therefore a cousin of the Lord. The *Golden Legend* records that Simon preached in Egypt and then proceeded with St. Jude to Persia, where notable miracles testified to the complete worthlessness of idols and so enraged the pagan priests that they rushed at the Apostles and hacked them to pieces. St. Simon's usual emblem is a fish, to show that he was a fisherman[4] or possibly to connect him with the miracle of the Feeding of the Five Thousand. But he may hold an oar, an axe, a saw, or even, through confusion with St. James the Less, a fuller's club.

[1] St. Matthew x. 4 = St. Mark iii. 18 = St. Luke vi. 15.
[2] i. 13.　　[3] St. Mark vi. 3; St. Matthew xiii. 55.
[4] Perhaps by confusion with Simon Peter (St. John xxi).

SITHA

Sitha (Zita) became a domestic servant in the household of the Fatinelli family at Lucca when she was twelve years old (A.D. 1230) and remained there until her death in 1278. Remarkable alike for piety and for conscientious industry, she at first had to endure suspicion and harsh treatment from her employers and her fellow servants alike, but came later on to be regarded with affection and high respect. St. Sitha is quite frequently shown in English churches as a young woman holding one or more of her emblems, which are a rosary, a (prayer) book, and a key or keys. Occasionally she has loaves instead, or a basket of fruit. The loaves may refer to a story told about her that one morning she continued her devotions until the sun was up, when, suddenly remembering that it was baking-day, she hastened in dismay to the kitchen. There, however, she found a row of loaves neatly set out and waiting to be put into the oven.

SIXTUS

Sixtus (Xystus) is very rarely to be seen in English churches; at Wiggenhall, Norfolk, he appears as a bishop with crozier and book. Two popes who bore this name are claimed as martyrs. Of the first Sixtus, who governed the church of Rome about A.D. 117–26, nothing is known. The second Sixtus was pope for the year 257–8. He strove to appease the quarrel which had broken out between Rome and the churches of North Africa over the question of the rebaptism of heretics, and met his death in a revival of persecution ordered by the emperor Valerian. Sixtus was arrested while seated in his episcopal chair, in the cemetery of Praetextatus, giving instructions to a body of Christians who had assembled there, and was beheaded immediately afterwards. Another account, derived from St. Ambrose,[1] records that, as Sixtus was being led away to trial and execution, his deacon, the famous St. Laurence, desired to accompany him but was told to attend to the proper disposing of the treasures of the church in the certainty that his own martyrdom would take place three days later.

[1] *On the Duties of the Clergy*, i. 41.

STEPHEN

Stephen, 'a man full of faith and of the Holy Spirit', was one of the seven deacons appointed to relieve the Apostles of administrative duties.[1] He 'wrought great wonders and signs among the people', thus arousing the opposition of certain Jews who accused him of blasphemy. When summoned before the Sanhedrin he made a fearless, and even provocative, speech which caused his infuriated adversaries to defy legality and stone him.[2] St. Stephen was therefore honoured as the first Christian to suffer martyrdom. He is shown dressed in the vestments of a deacon (alb and dalmatic), with stones in his hand or on a book.

[1] Acts vi. 1–6.   [2] Acts vii.

SWITHUN

Swithun was chosen by Egbert, king of the West
Saxons, as tutor to Prince Ethelwulf and, when
Ethelwulf succeeded to the throne, Swithun was appointed bishop of Winchester. Swithun and Ealstan,
bishop of Sherborne, were the king's chief counsel-
lors and, while Ealstan offered political advice,
Swithun concentrated on ecclesiastical matters and
is said to have secured the grant of considerable
revenues to the Church. He ruled his diocese with
simplicity and diligence, travelling on foot and by
night in order to avoid ceremony. He built or re-
paired a number of churches, constructed a stone
bridge across the river Itchen, and caused diocesan
records to be kept which later proved a valuable
source of information when the *Anglo-Saxon Chronicle*
was compiled. His considerate charity is illustrated
by the story that, when a market woman was jostled
by a ruffian and dropped her basket of eggs, Swithun
'blessed the eggs and they were made whole and
sound'.[1] He died in 862 and was buried in the grave-
yard on the north side of Winchester Cathedral, but
in 971 his body was translated to a noble shrine
within the Cathedral. The story that heavy rain,
lasting for forty days, impeded the transference of
the bishop's remains led to the belief that:

> St. Swithun's day, if thou dost rain,
> For forty days it will remain;
> St. Swithun's day, if thou be fair,
> For forty days 't will rain na mair.

St. Swithun's great popularity is attested by fifty-two

[1] *Golden Legend*, iv, p. 54.

ancient church dedications, but, curiously enough, he is seldom depicted, and then as a bishop with no distinctive emblem.

SYMPHORIAN

A native of Autun, in Burgundy, he was brought up as a Christian and suffered martyrdom in the reign either of Aurelius (A.D. 161–80) or Aurelian (A.D. 270–5). The provincial governor, Heraclius, was eager to encourage the Gallic townsfolk in their worship of Cybele and, when Symphorian refused to reverence the image of the goddess, he was arrested. Unmoved either by persuasion or by torture he was led outside the city and beheaded while his mother, standing on the city wall, exhorted him to remain firm in the certainty that he would pass through death to eternal life. St. Symphorian was highly honoured in France but little known in England, though the Cornish churches of Forrabury and Veryan are dedicated to him.

THADDAEUS

Thaddaeus is the name given by St. Matthew[1] and St. Mark[2] to the Apostle who is called 'Judas of James' by St. Luke.[3] The historian Eusebius makes him one of the Seventy Disciples[4] and gives a lengthy account of his mission to King Abgar of Edessa, but he is usually identified with St. Jude.

[1] xi. 3.   [2] iii. 18.   [3] vi. 16; Acts i. 13.
[4] St. Luke x. 1.

THEOBALD

Theobald (1017–66) was a wealthy young man of Provins, near Paris, who, feeling himself called to follow the example of the Desert Fathers, refused all opportunities of success as soldier or courtier, and, with one companion, retired to live a life of solitude in the forest of Pettingen, Luxemburg. The two hermits gained their bread by carrying out the humblest tasks of manual labour, but, becoming embarrassed by the attention which their reputation for sanctity was attracting, they set out on a pilgrimage to Compostella and thence to Rome. Finally they settled in remote cells near Vicenza where, after the death of his companion, Theobald devoted himself to unremitting prayer and extreme but cheerful asceticism. Another Theobald (1200–47) had a somewhat similar history, since he was a favourite knight at the court of King Philip Augustus II of France but gave up worldly prospects in order to become a monk at Vaux-de-Cernay. In time he was elected abbot and excelled in monastic virtues. A 'St. Theobald' is painted on a screen-panel at Hempstead, Norfolk, where, however, he is represented as a bishop with his right hand raised in benediction. This mistake is probably due merely to the artist's ignorance, but there may be some confusion with the Theobald who was archbishop of Canterbury 1139–61.

THEODORE

Theodore (A.D. 602–90), who had received an excellent education at Tarsus, his native city, and at Athens, became a monk at Rome and, at the age of sixty-five, was unexpectedly chosen by Pope Vitalian as archbishop of Canterbury. The English Church was at that time in a state of much confusion and vexed by personal rivalries, so that Theodore had an immediate opportunity of showing his talent for firm but sympathetic administration. Vacant sees were filled and, at a council held at Hertford in 673, the bishops pledged themselves to observe canons that helped to regulate 'godly discipline'. A few years later Theodore travelled northwards to intervene in the quarrel between King Egfrid of Northumbria and St. Wilfrid. He consecrated other bishops to take Wilfrid's place and about the same time was successful in reconciling Egfrid and his rival, the king of Mercia. Theodore continued his policy of reorganization by founding a number of new dioceses and stressing their dependence on Canterbury, while, towards the end of his long life, he arranged a compromise which allowed Wilfrid to return to Northumbria and assume a somewhat restricted episcopal jurisdiction. St. Theodore was little regarded in the Middle Ages but his name has been included in the calendar of the 1928 Prayer Book.

THOMAS

Thomas, one of the Twelve Apostles. Nothing is recorded about him in the New Testament, except by St. John. When the disciples were trying to deter Jesus from taking the risk of going to Bethany where Lazarus lay dead, Thomas burst out, 'Let us also go, that we may die with him',[1] and he is mentioned as putting a question to Jesus at the Last Supper.[2] But he is remembered chiefly for his refusal to credit the other disciples with having seen the Risen Lord that led to the reappearance of Jesus in order to persuade him to be 'not faithless but believing'.[3] The *Acts of Thomas*, composed in the third century, record that the Apostle was taken to India to act as carpenter for King 'Gundaphorus'. He preferred, however, to spend his time in mission preaching, almsgiving, and curing disease, and the fame of his miraculous achievements caused such a disturbance that he was arrested and run through with spears. St. Thomas therefore bears a spear as his emblem.

[1] St. John xi. 16.   [2] xiv. 4.   [3] xx. 24-9.

THOMAS À BECKET

Thomas à Becket of Canterbury (1118–70). His remarkable abilities justified a speedy rise to eminence: in 1154 he was appointed archdeacon of Canterbury and the next year Henry II made him chancellor of England. He enjoyed the close friendship of the king and showed himself especially capable at carrying into effect the political reforms which Henry devised, while he distinguished himself also for his vigorous intervention in foreign affairs and his prowess on the field of battle. In 1162 Becket was, much against his own inclinations, promoted to be archbishop of Canterbury, and thenceforth he dedicated his powers to the service of the English Church. The result was a series of protracted quarrels with the king and his supporters concerning the respective privileges of Church and Crown. Thomas was forced to spend much of his time in France and on his return, in the vain hope of effecting a reconciliation, he was assailed by four knights in Canterbury Cathedral and killed by blows from their swords. St. Thomas of Canterbury enjoyed great popularity in the Middle Ages and his shrine became a noted place of pilgrimage, but comparatively few representations of him remain in English churches since King Henry VIII ordered their destruction on the ground that 'Bishop Becket' was a traitor rather than a saint. When he appears it is usually as an archbishop without distinctive emblem, but he may have a sword or an axe.

THOMAS CANTELUPE

Thomas Cantelupe of Hereford lived from A.D. 1218 to 1282. His noble connexions, personal attractiveness, and ability as scholar and teacher caused him to be elected chancellor of Oxford University in 1262. Two years later he was promoted to be chancellor of England but was deprived of his position when the death of Simon de Montfort enabled Henry III to punish those who had supported the barons against the king. Thomas Cantelupe then returned to his lecturing at Paris and at Oxford, and after receiving a number of canonries and benefices, was appointed bishop of Hereford in 1275. Though welcomed as a favoured adviser by King Edward I, he devoted himself chiefly to the firm and careful administration of his remote diocese. However, a quarrel between himself and Archbishop Peckham led to Cantelupe's excommunication and he died in Italy whither he had gone in order to appeal to the Pope. His shrine in Hereford Cathedral became the scene of frequent miracles and he was canonized in 1320. St. Thomas of Hereford is occasionally depicted, as at Ross-on-Wye, in the vestments of a bishop but without distinctive emblem.

UNCUMBER

Uncumber (Wilgefortis) is shown in King Henry VII's Chapel, Westminster Abbey, as a woman with long hair and a full beard, holding a book and a T-cross. The story goes that she was the daughter of a king of Portugal and dedicated herself to a life of virginity. Her father disapproved and selected a suitor for her, whereat Uncumber prayed that she might become so unattractive as to repel him. She immediately grew a beard, with the desired result, but the king, in his vexation, caused her to be crucified.

URITH (HIERAETHA)

Urith is patron of the church at Chittlehampton and appears in early sixteenth-century glass at Nettlecombe, Somerset. Her legend resembles that of St. Sidwell in that it makes her slain, a victim of her stepmother's jealousy, by haymakers who were bribed to attack her with their scythes.

URSULA

Her romantic legend makes her a British king's daughter who desired to escape the attentions of a pagan prince. Together with eleven thousand handmaidens she travelled by way of Cologne and Basel to Rome, where 'Pope Cyriacus' received the pilgrims with honour and, perceiving in a dream that they were to suffer martyrdom, abandoned his high office and, followed by several other bishops, joined their company. All returned to Cologne, which was at that time besieged by the Huns: 'and when the Huns saw them they began to run upon them with a great cry, and araged like wolves on sheep, and slew all this great multitude'.[1] Ursula's beauty attracted the prince of the Huns, and she could have saved her life by accepting his proposal of marriage, but, when she declined, he shot her through with an arrow. St. Ursula is therefore shown as a princess, crowned, and holding an arrow or transfixed by arrows. Sometimes, as at Eye, Suffolk, she shelters her virgin companions under her cloak.

[1] *Golden Legend*, vi, p. 66.

VALENTINE

A Roman priest said to have been beheaded for fearlessly proclaiming his Christian faith before the emperor Claudius Gothicus (A.D. 270). Whilst in prison he caused the governor's blind daughter to receive her sight through his prayers. No English churches are dedicated to St. Valentine, but the Anglican calendar commemorates him on 14 February, a day held sacred to lovers because all birds were thought to pair then.

VEDAST

Vedast was chosen by Clovis as his first instructor in the Christian faith and was present at the baptism of the King of the Franks by St. Remigius. For some years he had lived a life of solitary contemplation, but when called upon by Remigius to become bishop of Arras, and later of Cambrai also, he undertook the task of patiently building up Christian life and organization in a district which had been thrown into confusion by the inroads of heathen tribes. His episcopate lasted from about A.D. 500 to 540. Vedast may have a wolf for his emblem, because he once came into a ruined church and saw a wolf hiding among the bushes. At the bishop's command the wolf fled away and was never seen again.

VERONICA

Veronica (Berenice) is traditionally identified with
the woman who had an issue of blood and was
cured by touching Jesus' garment.[1] According to
a medieval legend the emperor Tiberius was once
afflicted with a sore disease and sent an officer named
Volusianus to demand that Pilate should produce
Jesus who 'cured all manner maladies'. Pilate was
terrified, and asked for a short delay, during which
time Volusianus 'found an old woman named Veronica which had been familiar and devout with Jesu
Christ'. She told him about the Crucifixion, whereat
Volusianus was much disappointed, but Veronica con-
soled him by declaring 'as I bare a linen kerchief in
my bosom, our Lord met me . . . and demanded my
kerchief and anon he emprinted his face and figured
it therein. And if my lord [Tiberius] had beholden
the figure of Jesu Christ devoutly he should be anon
guerished and healed.'[2] Veronica refused to sell her
possession but accompanied Volusianus to Rome and
showed it to the emperor, who received it with reverence and honour, and was immediately healed.

[1] St. Matthew ix. 20.
[2] *Golden Legend*, i, p. 83. The story is derived from an
Appendix to the apocryphal *Acts of Pilate*. See M. R. James,
The Apocryphal New Testament, p. 157.

VICTOR

Victor suffered martyrdom at Marseilles about A.D. 304. His *Acts* relate that the emperor Maximian came to Marseilles in order to persecute the Church. Victor, who was an officer in the army, went about encouraging the Christians to stand firm, until he was arrested and put in prison. Here he suffered savage tortures, but succeeded in converting his warders to the Faith before his execution. St. Victor is not often represented in English churches. At Torbryan, Devon, he is shown in armour, holding a sword and a windmill, because he was crushed by millstones and then beheaded.

VIGOR

A native of Arras and disciple of St. Vedast, he was appointed bishop of Bayeux about A.D. 514 and was distinguished for the conscientious care with which he administered his diocese and for the zeal with which he built churches on sites formerly consecrated to pagan worship. St. Vigor's reputation was mainly local, but he has two dedications in England—Fulbourn, Cambridgeshire, and Stratton-on-the-Fosse, Somerset.

VINCENT

Vincent is the Spanish counterpart of St. Laurence, but in England never attained the popularity of the Roman deacon. The fact of his death during the persecution of Diocletian (about A.D. 303) is well established, but the story of his martyrdom, as it was handed down by the hymn-writer Prudentius, appears to have been liberally embellished. Vincent is said to have been deacon to bishop Valerius of Saragossa, and to have regularly preached and taught on behalf of the bishop, who suffered from a severe stammer. The governor Dacian committed both bishop and deacon to prison for their firm adherence to Christianity, and, while Valerius suffered the penalty of exile, St. Vincent was called upon to endure tortures of barbaric ingenuity. He is depicted as a deacon with an iron hook, to indicate his torments, or with cruets and a book.

WALSTAN

Walstan attained considerable fame, particularly in East Anglia, as patron-saint of husbandmen and of their beasts. The story goes that Walstan was of royal parentage but renounced his worldly prospects and went off to work as a farm-labourer at Taverham, Norfolk. Though sometimes rebuked for indiscriminate charity, he soon gained the affection of his employers on account of his cheerfulness and industry. Many gifts were offered him, but he would accept none except two calves, and these only because it was revealed to him that they were to bear him to his burial-place. One day, as he was at work in the fields, an angel appeared to warn him that his hour had come and, after praying that those farmers who in future visited his tomb should obtain their petitions, he died peacefully. In accordance with his instructions Walstan's body was placed on a cart and drawn across country by his own oxen to Bawburgh where, though his shrine has been destroyed, his well is still to be seen. St. Walstan is shown crowned and holding a scythe: the two oxen may appear at his feet. A few representations of his mother, 'St. Blida', crowned and holding a book, also occur.

WANDREGESIL

Wandregesil (A.D. 600–68) was marked out for distinction at the court of Dagobert I, king of the Franks, and his prospects were enhanced by a prudent marriage into a wealthy family. But both husband and wife felt the ascetic impulse and decided to live apart, dedicating themselves to the religious life. Wandregesil became a vagrant pilgrim and then settled for some years at a monastery in the Jura. But he returned to Rouen, where he was ordained, and then established the monastery of Fontenelle, renowned for the rigour of its discipline. He remained there as abbot for nearly twenty years, varying the routine of the contemplative life with courageous mission-preaching among rough and lawless folk in the neighbourhood. St. Wandregesil is seldom depicted in England, and has no characteristic emblem. The church of Bixley, Norfolk, is dedicated to him and formerly contained his image, to which pilgrimages were made.

WENCESLAS

The son of Wratislav, duke of Bohemia, Wenceslas (A.D. 907–35) was brought up in an atmosphere of studious piety under the influence of his grandmother, St. Ludmila. On the death of Wratislav, the pagan and nationalistic party gained the upper hand with the result that Ludmila was murdered; but, when Wenceslas came of age, he proclaimed that he intended to govern in accordance with the precepts and practices of the Christian faith. He fostered friendly relations with the emperor Henry I of Germany, whom he acknowledged as his overlord, and he strove to secure the welfare of his people by repressing disorder and building churches and schools. However, his policy found opponents among the discontented nobles, who emboldened his brother Boleslas to slay him and seize the throne. Wenceslas was soon acclaimed as a saint and martyr; his shrine at Prague became a noted place of pilgrimage and he was adopted as the patron of Czechs. He gained little popularity in England, but is portrayed very occasionally, as in a window of the vestibule at York Minster, as a king with no characteristic emblem.

WENDREDA

Wendreda is the patron-saint of March, Cambridge-shire, but her history is completely uncertain. It is supposed that she was either the foundress of the chapel at March or else was abbess of a small nunnery that appears to have existed there. Her body was placed in a golden shrine and venerated at Ely until it was stolen by Canute.

WERBURGA

Werburga was the daughter of Wulfhere, king of Mercia, and Ermenilda, of the royal house of East Anglia. Werburga was still a child when Wulfhere died and she was taken to dwell with her great-aunt St. Etheldreda at Ely. Here she took the veil, and her reputation for piety joined with common sense caused her to be chosen by her uncle, King Ethelred, to supervise some of the monastic foundations in Mercia. She seems also to have been for a short time abbess of Ely. The stories told about her are legendary commonplaces. One of the miracles concerns a flock of geese that was devastating the crops of the villagers of Weedon: Werburga drove the geese into a stable and, next day, they begged to be released and expressed penitence for what they had done. She is said to have died at Trentham, Staffordshire, about A.D. 700, but her body was finally transferred to a shrine at Chester. St. Werburga is shown as a crowned abbess, perhaps holding a church, but with no characteristic emblem.

WERSTAN

A monk who escaped with his life when Deerhurst Abbey was sacked by the Danes, perhaps about A.D. 950, and retired to a remote hermitage in the forest, where Malvern Priory was later established. The details of his life are wholly uncertain, but in panels of fifteenth-century glass at Malvern Werstan is shown as the founder of the monastery church and as suffering martyrdom.

WILFRID

Wilfrid was brought up at the court of King Oswy of Northumbria and at Lindisfarne, where he showed himself to be both scholarly and devout. A pilgrimage to Rome familiarized him with the customs of the Roman as opposed to the Celtic church and, when he returned to Northumbria, he found that Alchfrith, son of Oswy, shared his view about the superiority of the former. Under the patronage of Alchfrith he established monasteries that were to observe the Benedictine rule, and his vigorous arguments at the Council of Whitby (664) caused Oswy to determine that the Roman usage alone should be followed in his kingdom. Wilfrid was designated bishop of York but went to Gaul for consecration and, when he returned, found that Chad had been appointed in his place. However, Archbishop Theodore caused Chad to be deprived in 669 and Wilfrid obtained his diocese, which he administered with diligence and much splendour. The Cathedral of York and noble churches at Ripon and Hexham testified to his zeal as a builder. In 678 Wilfrid quarrelled with both king and archbishop because of a scheme to subdivide the unwieldy Northumbrian diocese: he felt bound to appeal to the pope, and spent much time in exile. One result of this estrangement was that he carried out some vigorous and successful mission-preaching both in Frisia and in Sussex. Finally, at the Council of the Nidd, in 705, a reconciliation was effected. The Roman party was by now far more powerful than the Celtic, and it was decided to follow Wilfrid's wishes and assign to him the bishopric of

Hexham together with the monastery of Ripon. The remaining four years of his life were occupied principally in arranging for the maintenance of his well-loved abbeys. St. Wilfrid has about forty-three ancient churches dedicated to him. He is shown as a bishop or archbishop, with no distinctive emblem. Another Wilfrid, who is portrayed in a window of the choir at York Minster, was educated at Whitby Abbey and became the faithful helper of John of Beverley, whom he succeeded as archbishop of York (A.D. 718–37). He is said to have been a painstaking and enthusiastic teacher of the Christian faith and to have enriched his cathedral with costly altar-vessels. He spent the last few years of his life in retirement at Ripon.

WILLIAM OF NORWICH

William of Norwich is said to have been an eleven-year-old boy, remarkable for his piety, who was crucified at Norwich during Holy Week, 1144, by some Jews who wished to ridicule the Passion of Christ. The body was hidden in a wood, but was discovered because the place where it lay glowed with heavenly light. It was buried in the Monks' Cemetery, and the tomb gained a local reputation as the scene of miraculous healings. St. William of Norwich is depicted on several East Anglian rood-screens. At Loddon he is shown as a boy nailed to a rough cross while Jews stand near by, mocking him. Elsewhere he holds a cross and nails or hammer and nails.

WILLIAM OF YORK

William Fitzherbert became treasurer and canon of York about 1135. Enjoying the support of King Stephen, he was chosen to be archbishop of York in 1142, but the election was disputed and the disappointed candidate, Henry Murdac, a Cistercian monk, obtained the influence of St. Bernard and the Cistercian Order in aid of his plea that the pope should expel William from his see. For five years William ruled the diocese, where his easy-going affability made him popular, but when, in 1147, Murdac was consecrated archbishop in his stead, he retired to pass his days in prayer and study with the monks of Winchester. On Murdac's death in 1153, Pope Anastasius IV reinstated William, whose return to York was marked by great popular enthusiasm. So large was the crowd that the wooden bridge over the Ouse collapsed, but owing, as it was thought, to William's prayers, no one was drowned. A month later William died suddenly and poison was suspected. This gave him the reputation of being a martyr and, since miracles were reported at his tomb, he was canonized in 1226. A window in the north-east transept of York Minster illustrates some of these miracles together with events in his life, but he is usually portrayed as an archbishop with no distinctive emblem.

WILLIBRORD

Willibrord was born about A.D. 658 and received his education at Ripon Abbey and in Ireland. Here he was influenced by the missionary enthusiasm of a Northumbrian monk named Egbert and decided to devote his life to the task of evangelizing north-western Europe. He set out in A.D. 690 and, after some early reverses, settled at Utrecht under the patronage of Pepin II. Willibrord was consecrated by Pope Sergius as first bishop of the new see of Utrecht and laboured with unremitting zeal at preaching, teaching, and establishing churches and schools. According to his biographer Alcuin he was 'noble of aspect, joyous in heart, a wise counsellor, a compelling speaker, upright in character, and vigorous in every work of God'. In his old age he retired to the monastery of Echternach which he had founded, and died there about A.D. 740. St. Willibrord failed to obtain the favour in England that he deserved, and, when portrayed, is shown as a bishop without characteristic emblem.

WINIFRED

A Welsh saint of the seventh century. Her late and legendary *Lives* record that she dedicated herself to prayer and contemplation and therefore repulsed the advances of a certain Prince Caradoc, who flew into a rage and struck off her head. Where she fell, at Holywell, Flintshire, a copious spring of water gushed forth that is still claimed to possess remarkable curative powers. According to the story, St. Winifred's head was reunited with her body and she later became abbess of the monastery of Gwytherin. She is represented as an abbess holding a sword or as bearing her head in her hands. Her statue in King Henry VII's Chapel, Westminster Abbey, shows her with palm-branch and book, while a head lies near her feet.

WINWALOE

First comes David, then comes Chad,
Then comes Winnol, roaring like mad.

This East Anglian jingle served as a reminder that the third of March, when rough weather is to be expected, was the feast day of St. Winwaloe, a Breton monk of Irish descent who established the famous monastery at Landevennec, near Brest. He gained fame on account of the rigour of his austerities and the potency of his prayers which, on one occasion, so strengthened the local fishermen that they were enabled to repel a greatly superior force of pirates. Several Cornish churches are dedicated to him, but his reputation spread far afield and there was formerly a priory of St. Winwaloe at Wereham, Norfolk. On the rood-screen at Portlemouth, Devon, he is shown as a venerable bearded figure, with a church on his shoulder.

WISTAN (WINSTON)

According to his legend, he should have succeeded his grandfather Wiglaf as king of Mercia when he was only a child (about A.D. 840). His claim to the crown was set aside on account of his youth, but he was treacherously stabbed, at Wistow, Leicestershire, by two partisans of his uncle Berferth, who was determined to remove a possible claimant to the throne. The body was revealed by the appearance over it of a column of light and was removed to Repton Abbey for burial.

WITHBURGA

Withburga was a daughter of Anna, king of the East Angles, and sister of St. Etheldreda and St. Sexburga. She was educated at Holkham, on the coast of Norfolk, and then established a nunnery at East Dereham in the same county. She seems to have passed her days peacefully as abbess of her small community. The story goes that at one time, when food ran short, two does appeared and provided sufficient milk to save the nuns from starvation. St. Withburga is therefore shown as a crowned abbess with two does at her feet or a doe leaping up at her.

WOLFRIDA (WULHILDA)

See EDITH OF WILTON. The church of Horton, Dorset, is dedicated to her.

WULFRAM

Wulfram was elected bishop of Sens in A.D. 683 but, two years later, retired to the abbey of Fontenelle to prepare himself for missionary work in Frisia. He was well received by King Radbod, who had been favourably impressed by the work and teaching of the English missionary St. Willibrord, though the king declined to cut himself off from his ancestors by accepting baptism that would take him to Heaven while they remained in Hell. St. Wulfram is said to have been successful in rescuing several children who were about to be sacrificed to pagan deities and in gaining a number of converts, including one of Radbod's sons. The length of his stay in Frisia is uncertain, but he returned eventually to Fontenelle and died there about 720.[1] The Lincolnshire churches of Grantham and Dorrington are dedicated to his honour.

[1] The dates, and many other particulars, in the account of Wulfram's missionary expedition are confused and unreliable.

WULFSTAN

Wulfstan became prior of Worcester, where he was distinguished for his strict asceticism combined with affable benevolence. In 1062 he was persuaded, much against his will, to accept the bishopric of Worcester, and thereafter devoted himself to the conscientious and unaffected discharge of his pastoral office. He took particular delight in the companionship of children and in the services of the Church. The Norman conquest was a bitter blow to Wulfstan, but he accepted it as a just punishment for the sins of the nation. Scorned by the Normans on account of his lack of learning and of polish, he was summoned by archbishop Lanfranc to Westminster to show cause why he should not be deprived of his see. According to a twelfth-century legend, Lanfranc called upon Wulfstan to deliver up his pastoral staff and ring. But Wulfstan, declaring that he had accepted the bishopric of Worcester at the bidding of Edward the Confessor and that he would resign the tokens of his office to none other than Edward, fixed his crozier into the stone of the Confessor's tomb, saying 'Take this and give it to whom it pleaseth thee.'[1] He then laid his episcopal vestments aside and sat apart with the monks. But no one could move the crozier, so Wulfstan was summoned and made his prayer to the Confessor, whereat 'the hard stone resolved and let the staff go out, as it had been soft earth or clay'.[1] William the Conqueror and Lanfranc were much abashed and restored Wulfstan to his see, which he retained until his death in 1095. When St. Wulfstan

[1] *Golden Legend*, vi, p. 39.

is shown, as in fifteenth-century glass at Oddingley, Worcestershire, he appears as a bishop without characteristic emblem.

ZACHARIAS

Zacharias, the husband of Elizabeth and father of John the Baptist, was a Jewish priest 'of the course of Abia'. He was punished with dumbness for his refusal to believe the message of the angel Gabriel that Elizabeth should bear a son; but, at the circumcision and naming of his child, 'his mouth was opened and his tongue loosed'[1] and he was inspired to utter the Benedictus, praising God and foretelling the advent of the Saviour. To St. Luke's narrative an apocryphal tradition[2] added that he was put to death in the Temple, by Herod's command, for refusing to disclose the whereabouts of his son, and he was therefore acclaimed by the Church Fathers as a Christian martyr. When Zacharias is depicted he may hold a priest's censer or else a lighted taper, because he prophesied that the 'dayspring from on high' would appear 'to give light to them that sit in darkness'.[3]

[1] St. Luke i. 64.
[2] First found in the *Protevangelium of James* about A.D. 150.
[3] St. Luke i. 78.

APPENDIXES

I. ANGELS, PROPHETS, AND SIBYLS

Accompanying the various saints in medieval windows or
on rood-screens there may appear angels, prophets, and,
though very rarely, sibyls, all testifying, in their diverse
fashions, to the majesty of God and the grandeur of His
plan of redemption.

Angels are shown, in such early examples of Christian
art as the mosaics of Sta Maria Maggiore at Rome, in
mortal form apart from the nimbus of glory around their
heads and the addition, usual but not invariable, of wings
to indicate that they are the appointed messengers who
descend from Heaven to communicate God's wishes to
mankind and ascend thither again when their ministrations on earth have been accomplished. But by the sixth
century, at any rate in the Eastern Church, both painting
and literature had come under the influence of those pas-
sages in Scripture which point to distinctions of rank and
function in the Heavenly Host. The book of Genesis[1]
records that *cherubim* were stationed 'at the east of the
garden of Eden' with flaming swords in their hands 'to
keep the way of the tree of life'. So, in King Solomon's
Temple, cherubim made of olive-wood overlaid with gold
stood before the inmost shrine, guarding the whole
breadth of it with their outstretched wings;[2] and, later,
the prophet Ezekiel, in his vision by the River Chebar,
saw the 'glory of the Lord' upheld by cherubim, winged,
'full of eyes round about', moving forward upon whirling,
fiery wheels.[3] These supernatural ministers of God 'who

[1] iii. 34. [2] I Kings vi. 27.
[3] Ezekiel x.

sleep not and guard the throne of His glory'[1] are mentioned in the New Testament Epistle to the Hebrews[2] and
become, in the Book of Revelation,[3] 'the four living
creatures having each one of them six wings and full of
eyes round about and within, and they have no rest day
and night, saying, Holy, holy, holy is the Lord God, the
Almighty, which was and which is and which is to come'.
The four living creatures of the Apocalypse derive their
characteristics not only from the cherubim but also from
the *seraphim* who appeared to Isaiah during his vision 'in
the year that king Uzziah died'.[4] The seraphim are described as six-winged attendants, poised above 'the Lord
sitting upon a throne' and voicing His praises continually
in antiphonal chant until one of them darts down like a
lightning-flash to purge away Isaiah's iniquity and thus
prepare him for his prophetic mission.

Archangels are not mentioned in the Old Testament,
but St. Paul speaks of 'the voice of the archangel' in connexion with the second advent of Christ[5] and, in the
Epistle of Jude, Michael, the champion and guardian of
Israel,[6] is called 'the archangel'. To such heavenly
beings—angels, archangels, cherubim, and seraphim—
might be added, by those eager to classify and define, five
other orders deduced from the language of St. Paul. In
his letter to the Ephesians,[7] the Apostle speaks of Christ
as being raised from the dead and established 'in the
heavenly places, far above all rule, and authority, and
power, and dominion, and every name that is named, not
only in this world, but also in that which is to come',
and, when instructing the church at Colossae about the
activity of Christ, he declares that 'in Him were all things
created, in the heavens and upon the earth, things visible

---

[1] The cherubim and seraphim are so described in the Jewish
'Parables of Enoch' that date from about 70 B.C.

[2] ix. 5. [3] iv. 8. [4] Isaiah vi. 1.
[5] 1 Thessalonians iv. 16. [6] Daniel xii. 1. [7] i. 21.

and things invisible, whether thrones or dominions or principalities or powers'.[1] There was thus a Scriptural basis for distinguishing nine orders in the celestial hierarchy, as was done, early in the sixth century, by an unknown scholar who produced a series of learned treatises under the pseudonym of Dionysius the Areopagite. The name of St. Paul's Athenian convert[2] bestowed upon these speculations an almost apostolic authority which led to their acceptance throughout the Christian world as a pattern of revealed truth which was reflected not only in the pictures of the Nine Orders of Angels that adorned many churches but also in the poetry of Dante and Milton. According to 'Dionysius', these nine choirs of angels were divided into three groups, the first ever remaining in ecstatic adoration around the throne of God, the second holding aloof from the contamination of mortal folly yet transmitting the divine illumination to the third and lowliest group whose members intervene actively in the working of the created universe and in the lives of men. The first group includes Seraphim, Cherubim, and Thrones, the second Dominions, Authorities (later known as Virtues), and Powers, the third Principalities, Archangels, and Angels. The medieval artist allowed his imagination to range freely about this heavenly hierarchy, and representations of the Nine Orders never became standardized, but the rood-screen at Barton Turf, Norfolk, offers a finely executed set of figures that may be taken as typical:

Seraphim. Six-winged, feathered body, swinging a censer.

Cherubim. Six-winged, feathered body marked with eyes, hands uplifted in adoration.

---

[1] Colossians i. 16. The list 'thrones, dominions, principalities, and powers' was taken, no doubt rightly, to refer to orders of angels rather than to dignitaries upon earth.

[2] Acts xvii. 34.

267

Thrones. Six-winged, holding a pair of golden scales.

Dominions. Four-winged, wearing a triple crown and a chasuble.

Virtues. Four-winged, body covered with blue feathers, holding a sceptre.

Powers. Holding a scourge and leading a devil tied by a chain.

Principalities. Four-winged, holding a palm-branch in one hand and a glass vial in the other.

Archangels. Two-winged, in armour, standing within a fortress and holding a sword.

Angels. In white robe, holding a spear. Nearby two naked souls kneel in supplication.

Owing to the spoliation of English churches, a full set of the Nine Orders of Angels is rarely to be found; but two or three of the Orders, with their names on scrolls underneath them, often remain in the small upper lights of Perpendicular windows.

Prophets. Scenes and figures from the Old Testament are quite frequently depicted, but the heroes of the Old Dispensation were honoured not so much for their own intrinsic merits and interest as because they indicated, in type and symbol, the glories that should, in God's good time, be manifested in Christ and the Christian Church. The Law, which had but 'a shadow of the good things to come',[1] appeared to St. Paul to be designed as 'a tutor to bring men to Christ',[2] and this view was taken over and elaborated in such works as the *Biblia Pauperum*— the 'Poor Man's Bible'—which, composed about 1300, achieved wide influence and popularity when printed editions began to circulate in the second half of the fifteenth century. Each page of this book provides three pictures, the two side ones portraying incidents of the Old Testament that foreshadowed the crowning event, drawn from the Gospel or the Acts of the Apostles, which

[1] Hebrews x. 1.   [2] Cf. Galatians iii. 24.

is placed in the centre. Thus, a picture of the Resurrection of Christ is flanked by representations of Samson bearing away the gates of the city of Gaza[1] and Jonah emerging from the mouth of the whale, while illustrations of Moses receiving the Law and of Elijah's sacrifice being consumed by fire accompany a picture of the Whitsun descent of the Holy Spirit. Moreover, medallions, forming part of the framework in which these scenes are set, contain figures of prophets who clasp scrolls displaying the mysterious words that found fulfilment only in the life of Christ and thereby witness to the harmony that underlies God's creation, wherein all piecemeal and partial revelation leads inevitably up to 'one far-off divine event'. In the same fashion the Twelve Prophets, when shown in English churches, as at Fairford, Gloucestershire, have no nimbus of glory shining round their heads and no emblems in their hands.[2] 'He who is least in the kingdom of heaven'[3] is greater than these; they are but precursors whose duty it is to show forth, on the scrolls which they display, those intimations of the full truth which had been revealed to them by divine inspiration. Their number and work answer, in the Old Dispensation, to those of the Apostles in the New, and they are therefore so arranged that each prophetic text may correspond with a sentence of the Creed inscribed on scrolls held by the Apostles. The order of the Apostles was established in the fifth century[4] and shows

[1] Judges xvi.
[2] Except that Isaiah occasionally has a saw, because of the tradition that he was sawn asunder by an impious partisan of King Manasseh. The Prophets are usually dressed in tunics, with mantles thrown over them. The head-dresses are often elaborate and adorned with pearls.
[3] St. Matthew xi. 11.
[4] It is first found in a sermon (number 240) assigned, though incorrectly, to St. Augustine and bearing the authority of his name.

little variation: that of the Prophets is not quite so regularly observed, but the Fairford windows give a normal sequence. First of the Apostles stands Peter, holding his keys: over his head is a scroll inscribed with the words 'Credo in Deum patrem omnipotentem creatorem coeli et terrae' ['I believe in God the Father Almighty, Maker of heaven and earth']. To him corresponds Jeremiah, with the text 'Patrem invocabitis qui fecit et condidit coelos' ['Ye shall call Him Father, who made and established the heavens'. iii. 19 and xxxii. 17]. Next comes Andrew, with his cross saltire and the sentence 'Et in Jesum Christum Filium eius unicum Dominum nostrum' ['And in Jesus Christ his only Son our Lord']. His prophetic counterpart is David, with the quotation from Psalm ii 'Dominus dixit, en filius meus es tu; ego hodie genui te' ['The Lord said, Lo thou art my son, this day have I begotten thee']. The order of the others is as follows:

iii. St. James the Great, in pilgrim's garb. 'Qui conceptus est de Spiritu sancto, natus ex Maria Virgine.' ['Who was conceived by the Holy Ghost, born of the Virgin Mary.']

Isaiah. 'Ecce virgo concipiet et pariet filium. ['Behold, a virgin shall conceive and bear a son.' vii. 14.]

iv. St. John, holding a chalice with a dragon emerging from it. 'Passus est sub Pontio Pilato, crucifixus, mortuus et sepultus.' ['Suffered under Pontius Pilate, was crucified, dead and buried.']

Zechariah. 'Suscitabo filios tuos.' ['I will raise up thy sons.' ix. 13. This text is ill-chosen: more usual is xii. 10. 'They shall look upon me whom they have pierced.']

v. St. Thomas, with spear. 'Descendit ad inferna, tertia die resurrexit a mortuis.' ['He descended into hell; the third day He rose again from the dead.']

Hosea (Oseas). 'O mors, ero mors tua; ero morsus

tuus, O inferne.' ['O death, I will be thy death; O hell, I will be thy sting.' xiii. 14.]

vi. St. James the Less, with fuller's club. 'Ascendit ad coelos, sedet ad dexteram Dei Patris omnipotentis.' ['He ascended into heaven, and sitteth at the right hand of God the Father Almighty.']

Amos. 'Qui edificat in coelum ascensionem.' ['Who buildeth an ascent up to heaven.' ix. 6.]

vii. St. Philip, with tall cross. 'Inde venturus est iudicare vivos et mortuos.' ['Thence He shall come to judge the quick and the dead.']

Zephaniah (Sophonias). 'Et accedam ad vos in iudicio et ero testis velox.' ['And I will come to you in judgement and will be a swift witness.' This text is not really from Zephaniah at all, but from Malachi iii. 5. The mistake seems to have been first made in manuscripts written about 1300 and was often repeated.]

viii. St. Bartholomew, with knife. 'Credo in Spiritum Sanctum.' ['I believe in the Holy Ghost.']

Joel. 'In valle Josaphat iudicabit omnes gentes.' ['In the valley of Jehoshaphat He shall judge all the nations.' iii. 12. More apposite and more commonly quoted is ii. 28. 'I will pour out my spirit upon all flesh.']

ix. St. Matthew.[1] 'Sanctam Ecclesiam Catholicam, Sanctorum communionem.' ['The Holy Catholic Church, the communion of Saints.']

Micah (Micheas). 'Invocabunt omnes eum et servient ei.' ['All shall call upon Him and shall serve Him.' Another mistaken attribution that is commonly repeated. The text is, in fact, drawn from Zephaniah iii. 9.]

[1] At Fairford a mistake has been made with this figure. It is unnamed and is identical with that of St. Thomas, both in emblem and text.

x. St. Simon, with saw. 'Remissionem peccatorum.'
['The forgiveness of sins.']

   Malachi. 'Cum odium habueris, dimitte.' ['When
thou shalt hate her, put her away.' ii. 16.]

xi. St. Jude,[1] with boat. 'Carnis resurrectionem.' ['The
resurrection of the body.']

   Daniel. 'Educam vos de sepulcris vestris, popule
meus.' ['I will lead you out of your sepulchres, O
my people.' Really from Ezekiel xxxvii. 12, but
easily confused with Daniel xii. 2.]

xii. St. Matthias, with halberd. 'Et vitam eternam.
Amen.' ['And the life everlasting. Amen.']

   Obadiah (Abdias). 'Et erit regnum Domini.
Amen.' ['And the kingdom shall be the Lord's.' 21.]

Sibyls. In the opinion of the early Church, it was not only
the Old Testament prophets to whom God had vouch-
safed a foreknowledge of the mystery of man's redemption. The philosopher Justin, writing as early as A.D. 150,
declared that 'all noble sayings, wherever uttered, belong
to us Christians',[2] by which he meant that the divine Word
had prompted 'chosen vessels' in every age to spell out
His message letter by letter and thus prepare mankind for
the full and final revelation in Christ. Plato, Cicero, and
other great figures of the pagan world came therefore to
be honoured as having forecast in dim outline truths
which the New Testament made abundantly manifest.
But, in the Middle Ages, the link between pagan and
Christian culture was maintained less by demonstrating
that the philosophers of Greece and Rome imply, in their
works, a system of Christian doctrine than by introducing
the Sibyls as the representative voices of classical antiquity.

The Sibyl, or 'wise woman' inspired by Apollo, had
become sufficiently well known by the fifth century B.C.

---

[1] At Fairford badly restored, and receives loaves of bread
instead of a boat.   [2] *Apology* II. 13.

for allusions to her in Greek comedy[1] to be readily appreciated. Her original home was in Asia Minor, but later on sibyls were multiplied, and the scholarly Varro, writing in Italy about 50 B.C., enumerates ten of them who had gained at any rate a local repute for their prophecies. Sibyls differed from oracles in that they did not offer information to any chance inquirer but burst suddenly into prophetic utterance under the incalculable impulse of the divine prompting. The most celebrated, at least for a time, was the Sibyl of Cumae, in Campania. According to Roman traditions she came from the East and took up her solitary abode in a vast cave hard by the temple of Apollo. When possessed by the spirit of prophecy she was so transformed as to strike all beholders with terror, but Aeneas was not thereby deterred from consulting her before he descended into the underworld.[2] Virgil, in his fourth Pastoral Poem, mentions the prophecies of the Cumaean Sibyl in connexion with his forecast of a Golden Age which was shortly to be ushered in by the birth of a child—perhaps a son of the consul Pollio—about whom he uses language that echoes the fervent Messianic hopes of Isaiah. It was, therefore, not unnatural that, from the time of Constantine onwards, this child was identified with Christ and Virgil acclaimed as a prophet whom the Sibyl had instructed to declare, in allegorical but significant imagery, the advent of the Saviour. Moreover, the extant Sibylline oracles appeared to be in harmony with this interpretation. The utterances originally assigned to the Sibyl of Cumae, which imported a note of mystical emotion into the cold formalism of Roman religion, were written, in hexameter verse, on palm-leaves and stored in the temple of Jupiter Capitolinus for consultation in time of distress or alarm. But they were destroyed by fire in 83 B.C. and, in order to repair this loss, envoys were

---

[1] Aristophanes, *Peace*, 1095, 1115.
[2] Virgil, *Aeneid*, vi. 45.

dispatched to various cities of Greece and Asia Minor in order to secure a new collection which, however, was allowed to remain in comparative obscurity and, after an unsuccessful attempt by the emperor Julian to revive interest in it, was publicly burnt at the beginning of the fifth century. But, before then, a curious medley of Jewish prophecies had usurped the title of 'Sibylline Oracles' and gained wide currency. These verses were composed at various times between about 150 B.C. and A.D. 270 and, having been worked over and added to in the Christian interest, were eagerly welcomed by later Christian apologists, who genuinely believed them to be pagan presages of the Gospel. Thus Lactantius, a learned rhetorician of North Africa, adopted the ten sibyls listed by Varro and ascribed to them prophecies, drawn for the most part from the 'Sibylline Oracles', which had found fulfilment in the life of Christ or could be readily applied to the Christian expectation of the Last Judgement.[1] Therefore, since the work of Lactantius was rediscovered and highly appreciated in the second half of the fifteenth century, some sets of sibyls, such as those which were carved on the choir-stalls at Ulm Cathedral about A.D. 1470, are shown as pronouncing oracles which Lactantius had put into their mouths. But the English examples, the sibyls which appear on several Devonshire rood-screens,[2] are differentiated by characteristic emblems drawn from other sources. In 1481 a Dominican friar named Filippo Barbieri produced a collection of short treatises, in one of which pagan sibyls and Jewish prophets are set side by side, in pairs, to proclaim the coming of the Redeemer. The number of the sibyls is increased to twelve, no doubt in order to correspond more exactly with the prophets, by the addi-

[1] *Institutiones Divinae* I, vi, where reference is made to Varro's researches.

[2] Bradninch, Heavitree, Ugborough, and (one sibyl only) Ipplepen.

tion of 'Sibylla Agrippa'[1] and 'Sibylla Europa'; their costume and appearance are carefully described and they utter strange predictions drawn not from the 'Sibylline Oracles' but from an unknown source—probably a collection of medieval prophecies current at that time in the monasteries of southern Italy. Barbieri's work exercised a notable influence on the art of western Europe and fixed the mode of portraying the twelve sibyls who are thenceforth usually shown bearing attributes which Barbieri's oracles, when refined in the alembic of a medieval theologian's imagination, had suggested. The sibyls painted on the screen-panels at Bradninch appear thus:

i. *Samia*, with cradle. She had prophesied 'Lo, a time will come when a child shall be born of a poor maiden, and the beasts of the earth shall adore Him.'

ii. *Erythraea*, with a rose. To her had been assigned an oracle which foretold the Annunciation, and the Annunciation is commonly symbolized by a flower.

iii. *Persica*, with lantern. She had prophesied the trampling down of the powers of evil, and is sometimes shown with a dragon at her feet. The lantern was added to show that she 'foretold the Saviour, but obscurely', and the light in the lantern is therefore merely a feeble glimmer.

iv. *Europa*, with sword. According to Barbieri, she had declared that Christ would 'come and cross mountains and hills and the streams of Olympus: He shall reign in poverty and rule in silence'. Medieval artists interpreted this as a reference to the Flight into Egypt,[2] and the sword recalls the Massacre of the Innocents which the Infant Christ escaped by His departure from Palestine.

v. *Agrippa*, with a scourge. Her prophecy which spoke,

[1] Probably a mistake for 'Aegyptiaca'—the 'Egyptian prophetess'.
[2] St. Matthew ii. 13.

in Johannine language, of the 'handling of the Word'[1] was misinterpreted as a reference to the Scourging.

vi. *Tiburtina*, with a hand. She was thought to have foretold the buffeting which Christ received at the hands of those who arrested Him.[2]

vii. *Libyca*, apparently with a chalice or ewer and basin. The more usual emblem is a candle, because this sibyl had proclaimed, 'Behold, God will come and will shine in the thick darkness.'

viii. *Hellespontica*, with a cross. She had announced Christ's birth of a Virgin and His death on 'a cross high lifted-up'.

ix. *Cumana*, with a sponge. On the Continent she sometimes holds a basin. Both emblems seem to have originally referred to the washing of the new-born Babe, whose advent she had foretold in language drawn from Virgil's fourth Pastoral Poem—'now a new Son is sent down from the lofty heaven'.[3] But the English artists seem rather to have had in mind the sponge which was 'filled with vinegar and put on a reed' and offered to Christ when He was on the cross.[4]

x. *Cimmeria*, with horn. Barbieri put into her mouth a prophecy that 'a fair Virgin would nourish her Son, giving Him milk to drink'. The horn is a feeding-bottle.

xi. *Delphica*, with pincers and nails. She usually holds a crown of thorns, because she had declared that Christ would fall into 'the hands of impious men and be crowned with a crown of thorns'.

xii. *Phrygia*, with cross and banner. She was held to have prophesied the Resurrection, of which the cross and banner is a common symbol.

The names of the sibyls are not given on the English

---

[1] 1 John i. 1.   [2] St. Luke xxii. 63.
[3] Virgil, *Eclogue*, iv. 7: Iam nova progenies caelo demittitur alto.   [4] St. Matthew xxvii. 48.

screens and have therefore to be deduced from those French and Italian figures[1] which are accompanied by both names and emblems.

II. AN ALPHABETICAL LIST OF EMBLEMS AND A NOTE ON VESTMENTS

Anchor. Clement (pope).

Angel. Matthew.

Anvil. Adrian.

Armour. Armel (chasuble worn over armour). Donatus (with crozier). George. Jeron (cassock worn over armour). Maurice. Michael (archangel). Victor.

Arrow or arrows. Christina. Edmund (king). Sebastian. Ursula (crowned).

Asperge (an holy-water vessel). Martha.

Auger. Leger (bishop).

Axe or halberd. Alphege (bishop). Matthias. Olave (king). Thomas of Canterbury (archbishop).

Bag or purse. Matthew.

Basket. Dorothy (basket of flowers and fruit). Philip (basket of loaves).

Beard. Uncumber (shown as a woman with a full beard).

Bedstead. Faith.

Beggar. Martin (sharing cloak with a beggar or giving alms to a beggar).

Bell. Antony.

Boat. Jude. Nicholas (bishop).

Book. Not a distinctive emblem. It is borne by the Four Evangelists and by such learned persons as Ambrose, Augustine, Bede, Catharine of Alexandria, Gregory, and Jerome. But it is not confined to them and may be

[1] Although the assignment of a fixed emblem to a particular sibyl is generally observed on the Continent, slight variations occur from place to place.

held by bishops, and indeed, by any saint who spread the Gospel abroad or whose life reflected the Gospel precepts.

Bottle. See *Phial.*

Breast. Agatha (breast in a pair of pincers or sword through breasts).

Calves. Walstan (crowned, with calves at his feet).

Candle. Geneviève.

Cardinal. Jerome often appears in cardinal's robes and hat.

Carpenter's square. Matthew.

Chain. Leonard (abbot). Ninian (bishop). Peter.

Child or children. Anne (teaching her child, the Virgin Mary, to read). Christopher (carrying the Christ-child across the river). Mary of Clopas (with four sons). Mary Salome (with two sons). Nicholas (bishop with three boys).

Church. There is nothing distinctive about this emblem: it may be borne by any founder of a cathedral or parish church.

Cloak. Martin (divides it with a beggar). Ursula (crowned, shelters her companions under her cloak).

Club. James the Less. Jude. Simon.

Coals. Brice (bishop carrying coals in a vestment).

Comb. Blaise (bishop).

Cross. This is not a distinctive emblem; indeed a tall cross-staff is regularly borne by any archbishop. But a cross is particularly associated with Alban, Andrew (cross saltire), Gregory (Christ crucified appears on the altar before which Gregory kneels), Helen (crowned), Louis (king), Margaret (thrusts the staff of a cross into a dragon's mouth), Philip, William of Norwich (boy with cross and nails or crucified).

Crown of thorns. Catharine of Siena. Louis (king).

Cruets on a book. Vincent (deacon).

Cup. Edward (king). John the Apostle (with dragon emerging from the cup).

Dagger. Edward (king).

Devil. Benedict (repelling devils with his crozier). Dunstan (a bishop seizing the devil with pincers). John Schorne (holds a boot with the devil emerging from it). Juliana (flogs the devil or leads the devil by a chain).

Dish. Oswald.

Doe or does. Giles (abbot). Withburga (royal abbess).

Dog. Bernard (abbot).

Dove. Gregory (pope).

Dragon. Armel (leads the dragon by a' stole). George. John the Apostle (cup with a dragon emerging from it). Margaret (thrusts the staff of a cross into a dragon's mouth). Michael (archangel in armour striking down a dragon).

Eagle. St. John the Apostle.

Eyes on a book. Lucy.

Falcon. Jeron.

Fetters. Leonard (abbot).

Fish. Eanswith (royal abbess). John of Bridlington. Kentigern (fish with ring in its mouth). Simon.

Flowers. Cecilia (garland of flowers). Dorothy (basket of flowers). Louis (*fleurs-de-lis*).

Goose or geese. Martin (bishop). Milburga (abbess).

Gridiron. Faith. Laurence (deacon).

Hair, flowing. Mary Magdalene. Mary of Egypt.

Halberd. See *Axe.*

Hammer. Eloy (bishop).

Handkerchief, with portrait of Christ imprinted upon it. Veronica.

Head, carried in the hands or lying on the ground. Denis (bishop). Oswald (his crowned head in St. Cuthbert's hands). Osyth. Sidwell. Winifred.

Heart, burning. Augustine of Hippo (bishop). Catharine of Siena.

Hind. See *Doe.*

Hook. Vincent (deacon).

Horn. Cornelius (pope).

Inkhorn. Jerome (cardinal).

Key or keys. Peter. Petronilla. Sitha.

Knife. Bartholomew. Peter Martyr (knife in head).

Ladder. Alexis.

Ladle. Martha.

Lamb. Agnes. Joachim. John the Baptist.

Lance. See *Spear.*

Lantern. Gudule.

Lily. The Virgin Mary.

Lion. Jerome (cardinal). Mark.

Loaf or loaves. Elizabeth of Hungary (crowned). Mary of Egypt (with flowing hair). Olave (king). Philip. Sitha.

M. The letter M with a crown over it is the badge of the Virgin Mary.

Mice on her crozier. Gertrude (abbess).

Monstrance. Clare (abbess).

Nails. Louis (king with cross and nails). William of Norwich (child with cross and nails).

Oar. Julian Hospitaller. Simon.

Ox. Luke. Walstan (crowned, with oxen at his feet).

Palm. Not a distinctive symbol. It is frequently borne as a sign of martyrdom, particularly by virgin martyrs, being suggested by Revelation vii. 9, where a great and triumphant multitude stands 'before the throne and before the Lamb, arrayed in white robes and palms in their hands'.

Phial, glass. Cosmas and Damian.

Pig. Antony.

Pilgrim. St. James the Great (with staff, wallet, and scallop-shell). Roch (pilgrim pointing to a plague-spot on his thigh).

Pincers. Agatha (holds her breast in a pair of pincers). Apollonia (holds a tooth in a pair of pincers). Dunstan (seizing the devil with pincers).

Plague-spot. Roch (points to a plague-spot on his thigh).

Pot of ointment. Cosmas and Damian. Joseph of Arimathaea. Mary Magdalene.

Raven. Paul of Thebes.

Ring. Edward the Confessor (king).

Rosary. Sitha.

Rose. Elizabeth of Hungary.

Saw. Simon.

Scales. Michael.

Scourge. Guthlac.

Scythe. Sidwell. Walstan (crowned).

Shield, with 'Ave Maria' engraved on it. Gabriel.

Shovel. Honorius (bishop).

Spear. Longinus (soldier). Oswin (king). Thomas.

Spinning-wheel. Geneviève.

Staff, budding. Joseph of Arimathaea.

Stag, with crucifix between its horns. Eustace. Hubert (bishop).

Stigmata (wounds in hand, feet, and side). Francis.

Stone or stones. Alphege (bishop). Stephen (deacon).

Swan. Hugh (bishop).

Sword. A general emblem of martyrdom, but borne in particular by: Agatha (sword through breasts), Agnes (sword through neck), Alban, Catharine of Alexandria, Lambert (bishop), Lucy (sword through neck), Matthew, Pancras (boy with sword and book), Paul, Thomas of Canterbury (archbishop), Victor (in armour).

Taper. Geneviève. Zacharias.

Tooth. Apollonia.

Tower. Barbara.

Vase. See *Pot of ointment.*

Veil, with portrait of Christ imprinted on it. Veronica.

Wheel, spiked. Catharine of Alexandria.

Windlass. Erasmus (bishop).

Windmill. Victor.

Wolf. Vedast (bishop).

Since some emblems were the common property of two or more saints, vestments, which the medieval artist usually depicted with great accuracy, may help towards the identification of the figures.

Bishops are nearly always shown wearing full eucharistic vestments which represent an adaptation of the costume in vogue at Rome during the early years of the Christian era. At that time the ceremonial was often splendid and the churches lavishly embellished, but the ministers were content to dress in the fashion observed by the laity. However, the clergy retained this dignified costume, enriching it with symbolical meaning, whilst civil dress underwent gradual change, and thus their apparel, somewhat modified to accord with liturgical usage, came to be entirely distinctive. The bishop therefore appears wearing a chasuble, originally a travelling-cloak but now shortened and bedecked with embroidery, over tunicle and dalmatic, two vestments, of similar pattern, reaching just below the knees and not very conspicuous under the chasuble. Below the edge of the tunicle the fringed ends of the stole are to be seen, and the maniple, originally a handkerchief, hangs over the left wrist. Round the neck appears a decorated collar which is the visible part of the amice, a linen napkin worn to protect the outer vestments from contact with the skin. But the obviously characteristic marks of a bishop, as opposed to a priest, are the mitre and the crozier. The mitre developed slowly from a conical helmet worn during outdoor processions into the high-pointed and bejewelled head-dress of the fourteenth century: the crozier, which is no more than an ornamented shepherd's crook, indicates that the bishop is the chief pastor in his community.

The *Archbishop* is distinguished from the bishop in two respects. He holds the cross-staff, originally the processional cross which was solemnly borne before him, instead of the crozier. And, worn over his chasuble, appears the pallium, a narrow fillet of wool, ornamented with crosses, which hangs from his shoulders in the shape of a letter Y. This pallium was originally an ample outer garment, like the Roman toga, but was reduced to a narrow band by folding and came to be a mark of honour bestowed as a personal gift by the Pope.

Popes are recognizable by the tiara, another development of the conical cap from which the mitre evolved. Unlike the mitre, it retained its antique shape but with bands of rich decoration added until, by about A.D. 1340, it had been transformed into a majestic head-dress encircled by three golden coronets.

Deacons (who in the earliest age of the Church were administrators of great authority and importance) wear a dalmatic over an alb. The dalmatic, which can now be seen since there is no chasuble to cover it, appears as an ornamented tunic with fringed slits up each side to the waist. In English churches the only saints who are likely to be shown vested as deacons are Laurence, Stephen, and, much more rarely, Vincent.

Monks. The earliest monastic vestment, adopted by both monks and nuns in Egypt, was the cowl, a rough cloak with a hood, which was commonly worn by peasants and slaves and therefore by the monks, most of whom were of humble birth. The appropriateness of this garment, as signifying lowliness and simplicity, soon came to be stressed, and its use was prescribed by St. Benedict for his communities in western Europe. During their hours of manual labour the Benedictine monks substituted the scapular, originally a workman's short blouse, for the cowl, either garment being worn, as monastic costume became standardized, over a long, sleeved habit, variously coloured to distinguish the Orders one from another.

Abbots, though sometimes represented in full eucharistic vestments and, in that case, resembling bishops, more often appear as monks, distinguished only by the crozier that betokened their pastoral authority over the monastery and its members. Abbesses also are shown holding a crozier and, when of royal lineage, they wear a crown.[1]

[1] The three most commonly so depicted in England are Bridget of Sweden, Etheldreda, and Withburga, but none is of frequent occurrence.

EACH figure of a saint in an old church, in stone or glass or on the carved screen, usually represents some particular person, but they are rarely named and the interested visitor without a guide-book usually cannot identify them. St. George and the Dragon, and a few others, are well known, but in medieval craftsmanship many other saints also had some emblem or object as a regular accompaniment in windows and carvings. This is a book of more than 250 saints, including all common and many uncommon ones, each of whom is connected in some way with at least one English church. It tells briefly who each was in fact or legend and, where there is an emblem by which the saint can be identified, gives this information. The commonest emblems are illustrated by small drawings.